'If you have ever uttered the phrase "there's no such thing as a rape culture", you need to read this book. If you believe that "women lie all the time" just to get revenge or out of guilt over sex, you need to read this book. If you think men are being unfairly accused by women and that the system is predisposed against them "because feminism", you need to read this book.'

Clementine Ford,
Sydney Morning Herald

'Just finished this in tears, full of admiration. Bri Lee's story of standing up for herself and braving a biased, underfunded, incompetent legal system to demand justice is beautifully written, tender and powerful. Accompanying Lee through her transformation from a frightened girl into a blazingly formidable adult— whose courage comes from her determination to stand up for all women—was moving, gut-churning, and ultimately triumphant. I punched the air when I finished. RESPECT.'

Charlotte Wood,
author of *The Natural Way of Things*

'Brutal, brave and utterly compelling, Bri Lee's extraordinary memoir shines a light on the humanity and complexity of our justice system and the limitless courage victims of crime must summon in a legal process stacked against them at every turn. In the age of #MeToo, *Eggshell Skull* is a prescient personal account of a young woman's fierce and unflinching battle against her abuser. I can't remember a book I devoured with such intensity, nor one that moved me so profoundly.'

Rebecca Starford,
author of *Bad Behaviour* and co-founder of *Kill Your Darlings*

'An illuminating meditation on society's complicity in sexual assault, told through one woman's pursuit of justice in a system that has failed women and survivors for too long. Powerful as it is timely, *Eggshell Skull* is a courageous, heartbreaking and ultimately hopeful memoir from one of Australia's sharpest young writers.'

Liam Pieper,
author of *The Toymaker*

'*Eggshell Skull* is as finely wrought as its name suggests—a sensitive and clear-eyed account of childhood sexual abuse that ripples out to encompass both its psychic aftershocks and the gruelling work of seeking legal redress. Lee doesn't flinch from the ugliness of the crime, but her eye for detail is always compassionate, never gratuitous. This is a book that honours its survivors, and one that should establish Lee as a serious name in Australian nonfiction.'

Jessica Friedmann,
author of *Things That Helped*

'*Eggshell Skull* is a page-turner of a memoir, impossible to put down . . . A great book with which to open a conversation about sexual assault and the way in which the legal system has let women down for too many years. If you are confused or disturbed by the sudden upsurge of #MeToo accusations, *Eggshell Skull* will give you an insight into the anger and vitriol of many survivors.'

Krissy Kneen,
author of *An Uncertain Grace*

Beauty

Bri Lee is an author and freelance writer. Her journalism has appeared in publications such as *The Monthly*, *The Saturday Paper*, *Guardian Australia* and *Crikey*. Her first book, *Eggshell Skull*, won Biography of the Year at the ABIA Awards, the People's Choice Award at the Victorian Premier's Literary Awards, and was longlisted for the 2019 Stella Prize. She is also a non-practicing lawyer and continues to engage in legal research and issues-based advocacy.

Beauty

Bri Lee

ALLEN&UNWIN
SYDNEY·MELBOURNE·AUCKLAND·LONDON

First published in 2019

Allen & Unwin
83 Alexander Street
Crows Nest NSW 2065
Australia
Phone: (61 2) 8425 0100
Email: info@allenandunwin.com
Web: www.allenandunwin.com

 A catalogue record for this
book is available from the
National Library of Australia

ISBN 978 1 76087 652 4

Set in 12/18.4 pt Baskerville MT Pro by Bookhouse, Sydney
Printed and bound in Australia by Griffin Press, part of Ovato

10 9 8 7 6 5 4 3 2 1

For all the people who wrote to me after
Eggshell Skull *saying it made them feel*
a little stronger within their own bodies.

THE HOUSE I rented through 2017 was the first place I had ever lived or even stayed in for an extended period of time where I had never thrown up after dinner. In February 2018 my partner and I signed a twelve-month lease renewal on this happy home, but it was not an anniversary I felt inclined to celebrate. Was I exhibiting more, or less, self-control by resisting the urges? In the weeks and months that followed I began thinking a lot about vomiting again. Or, rather, I longed to purge again. The craving for the small ritual grew both in frequency and intensity as the publication date and publicity tour of my first book approached.

Marcus Aurelius wrote about self-discipline as the source of contentedness. His book *Meditations* was written for nobody but himself; it is self-exploration at its most pure. If Aurelius were a woman instead of a famous stoic philosopher-emperor we might describe *Meditations* as a diary. Reading his work, I was drawn to the idea that the only thing I could control was myself, and that the rest of the world was an unpredictable source of agony and exhilaration I must simply accept and do my best within. 'In a mind that is disciplined and purified there is no taint of corruption, no unclean spot nor festering sore,' he stated, and exhorted himself to: 'Erase fancy; curb impulse; quench desire; let sovereign reason have the mastery.'

My trouble was that I couldn't control myself. Maintaining mastery over my emotions was the path to finally feeling satisfied and happy with myself, but hunger was an emotion I couldn't control and if I didn't master hunger the self-loathing arrived on its heels like clockwork. Gut-churning from no food was the harbinger of belly-gurgling with guilt in fullness. I didn't realise how bad my disordered eating habits were until I finished the first draft of my memoir and found it pushing itself to the surface of every single chapter. When I was editing that book I tried to remove those segments, out of shame and embarrassment, but ultimately I put them back in, realising how important they were to a story that was so much about deciding my own worth in the world.

Obsession with thinness is an embarrassing admission. As a well-educated young woman who tries to engage in deep thoughts, admitting to caring so deeply about your figure is tantamount to saying you would choose Barbie dolls over chemistry sets all over again. The memoir was set in a time when I was working in a big, important job, surrounded by high achievers. People who habitually ran half

3

marathons on weekends as a 'hobby'. You were either fit and trim or you just weren't working hard enough. Your body was how you conveyed wealth and status to your peers, it was a personality trait, a symbol of goodness and values: an ethical ideal.

So the question I found myself asking in April, as I stared at the bottom of the shower past a belly expanded with dinner, was whether or not I was more like Marcus Aurelius if I stuck my fingers down my throat, or more like Marcus Aurelius if I didn't. 'What do the baths bring to your mind? Oil, sweat, dirt, greasy water, and everything that is disgusting,' he wrote, and I knew what he meant. The body is so easily grotesque. At 64 kilograms I was smack bang in the middle of the 'normal' BMI range. To a determined young woman with dreams bigger than Brisbane, 'normal' wasn't great. Not Marcus Aurelius great. Not lean-and-driven, specimen-of-a-human-in-their-prime great. He asked of me, 'What is the very best that can be said or done with the materials at your disposal?'

The matter was made more complex by the knowledge that I was once 57 kilograms, right on the borderline of an 'unhealthy' BMI. I wore sample size clothes, people complimented me on how good I looked, and I was told by a modelling scout that I was only 'just a little too big' to try for the catwalk professionally. I stood under the hot water and watched it bounce off my breasts. In thinner times they had shrunk to a B cup, protruding only an inch further than my clavicles. Once, when I was about 70 kilos, my breasts had practically tumbled out of the cups of my bras because I refused to buy bigger ones and therefore accept my size. I did not share my boyfriend's enthusiasm about this. In fact, he would probably find it easier to be my boyfriend if I was a little less determined to transcend my body.

'Would you still love me even if I was really fat?' I asked him once.

'Yes,' he replied.

This couldn't be good. Was it possible his almost-unconditional love was holding me back? The sinusoidal trip was this: his love made me feel accepted, content and complacent, but the complacency meant I did not strive, and I did not know how to be happy with myself when I was not striving. How could I like myself if I was not measuring constant improvement? How could I respect myself if I was slowing or stalling, even stagnating?

'I just want to lose two kilos,' I mentioned another time.

'I know how this goes. You lose two and then you want to lose another two and you keep going until you get to zero,' he said.

That sounded pretty good to me.

Before I decided to share my life with him I was significantly more productive but also much more regularly and intensely miserable. My habit was to take that inward hate and convert it into kinetic energy. The misery of the night before would push the run the following morning. The terror of celebrating a birthday in December without tangible career milestones to point to was what kept me awake past midnight, meeting deadlines, in October. Self-improvement without self-loathing seemed impossible. In life you had to be both the horse and the jockey: whipping and giving directions while your own lungs filled with blood.

In choosing love I had chosen happiness over achievement in the same way I had, one hour before that shower in April, chosen a burger and beer over salad and vodka for dinner. Every single mealtime presented me with the question: *What kind of woman do you want to be?* When my boyfriend was with me at the restaurant the philosophical thoughts were covered in a kind of fog. I saw the happy face of my lover

7

instead of Marcus Aurelius. A diffusing effect of his love, and of our life together. We made each other laugh.

'I don't know what to order,' I said.

'What do you feel like?' he replied.

Was it really that simple?

•

THE QUESTION I asked myself at the end of each long run was the same question I asked at the end of each draft of my first manuscript: *This is okay, but what am I truly capable of?* If only I worked harder, maintained more focus, spent less time with friends and loved ones, what heights could I reach? What are any of us truly capable of? What is the literary equivalent of 100 metres under ten seconds? Mostly I told myself this: If I was satisfied with my work I wouldn't be so hungry all the time. If I was fulfilled I wouldn't need so much filling. All eating was emotional eating. I couldn't seem to rise above it, and I wouldn't fulfil my true potential until I could. As I wavered in supermarket aisles or faltered when reading menus I would hear Aurelius: 'Is it this that I cannot resist?'

•

I WROTE A memoir in which my anxiety and self-loathing manifested in disordered eating, then a glossy women's fashion magazine invited me to Sydney for a glamorous photo shoot. That's funny, isn't it? I think it's funny. I was laughing at home alone into my vodka lime soda when I found out, so there was definitely something funny happening to me.

Through April I spoke to my publicist on the phone at least once a week and we emailed constantly. Extracts, interviews and photo shoots were being lined up to coincide with the book's publication in June. Photos of me and the book were starting to circulate on social media, and notifications that I had been tagged in new images filled my phone, interrupting my day with kicks of both anxiety and dopamine.

On my weekly grocery shopping trip I detoured into the newsagent to buy a copy of the magazine in which my photograph was to appear; the glamorous shoot was for a portfolio called 'Visionary Women' and it would feature eight of us in all, including women whose drive and intellect I deeply admired. I found the latest edition and got excited, but when I took the magazine to the counter I felt suddenly embarrassed and couldn't make eye contact with the sales assistant. In my old blue jeans and sneakers, with no make-up and my oily hair frizzing out the sides of my ponytail, I clearly had no business buying a publication of that kind.

'I'm going to be *in* this!' I wanted to say to him, to justify myself, but I was already gone, back in the warm, dusty safety of my car, tracing my fingers around the edges of the cover girl's silhouette. Georgia Fowler was the model;

'Modern Muse' the cover called her. That's what I was supposed to be—a demigoddess whose beauty inspired great art. The flesh of her upper arms dipped back in toward the bone after her elbows jutted out. I already followed her on Instagram and remembered seeing a video of her training at a gym I also followed on Instagram called Skinny Bitch Collective, or SBC, infamous for granting membership only to the already-trimmest-of-trim women. They even had to dress a certain way, in long black leggings and a crop top, their exposed abs being the critical component of the uniform.

My mobile pinged with another notification and, with the magazine on my lap and Instagram open on the phone in my hand, I had entered new territory. Coordinates were overlapping. My world was colliding with theirs, the collision allowing for vastly intensified comparisons. Those women in that perfect, parallel universe were real, their bodies corporeal and

11

therefore achievable. I was going to be in photos next to people paid to be beautiful in those pages, then made perfect by technology. Would I be airbrushed? Did I want to be airbrushed? The edition I was flipping through had articles on 'Face Shaving' and 'Next-Gen Needles'. It was the 'Beauty Issue'. Weren't they all beauty issues?

Backpedalling, I considered calling my publicist and declining the photo opportunity, scuttling back into the comfortable shadows of my own small orbit, but then, as I kept flipping, I got into it all again. One of my artistic heroes, the musician St Vincent, was modelling for Tiffany & Co. I'd admired her for years, fantasised about edging closer to her awesomeness in some way. She was obviously thin, coming *in* at the cheeks whereas I still went *out* at the cheeks. Keira Knightley was still advertising Chanel. Calvin Klein was reusing old images of Kate Moss, the first and original 'heroin chic' model, a resource so very over-tapped I just rolled my eyes. In one of the photos she was naked, like you needed a reminder that they were selling you dreams not jeans. Outrageous Versace with gold links and Medusa heads! Imagine all the cocaine behind the scenes. Maybe that's what I'd been missing—it's hard to get super thin without uppers of some kind. Then there was supermodel Gisele Bündchen. She and husband Tom Brady had their own chef, I learned, and 80 per cent of their diet was vegetables, mostly raw. The more I read, the more I believed I was looking at beautiful people. They seemed so rich and delightful, their lives and belongings rendered luminous in luxurious technicolour textures. Who wouldn't want to live like this? These people were travelling the world, making art, getting paid vast sums of money to be good-looking.

In the 'street style' section I spotted an influencer I'd met when I interned at New York Fashion Week a few years ago. During that fortnight I saw countless models changing back-stage for fittings and shows, and I never got used to it. They were so thin their thighs were barely larger than their calves. Apparently one of the big design houses' 'fit models'—the people whose bodies the clothes are measured, cut and sewn for—actually had a genetic condition that meant she had tiny bottom ribs, making her torso especially minute. The girls all groaned when they heard this, wondering how they could compete with such an advantage.

On the next page there was a photo from Dries Van Noten's latest show. I couldn't wait to watch the documentary about him that had just been released, to get a glimpse inside his magic world. He was one of my favourite designers; he claimed to design for the kind of woman who 'just goes for it' and was a master at the ugly-beautiful balance that keeps all of life, and art, interesting. It was exhilarating to think little old me in the supermarket car park might one day be in the same magazine as Dries' dresses.

Georgia Fowler talked about having a trainer in New York and a coach in Sydney. I wanted to hate her but I couldn't. A half-second of self-awareness revealed the truth of my envy. In the images she appeared so comfortable in her skin, so confident and at ease. Her father was a pro golfer. She walked in a Victoria's Secret show after her fifth audition. I yearned to remake myself in her image, and that's when it hit me once more: the determination, the churning, the striving. 'My diet does depend on what I have coming up,' she revealed. 'If I am being strict, I'll limit my sugar intake, so I'll limit fruit and I don't eat dairy because I don't think it's that good for you or reacts well with me personally.'

The more I read the more afraid I became. Afraid that I was nothing if I stopped trying to be the best. Anyone could be a regular shape, and everything I'd been taught about creation and personality and art-making was that you'd never get anywhere important if you were happy doing more of what has always been done. It was true that when I was busy—when I was whipped up, creating, caught in a whirlwind of work—I was less hungry, less reliant on food to fill me.

Another notification on my phone, this time a text from my publicist—*The shoot has to happen before 5 June*—and I resolved to try again, the fear and loathing calcifying into a schedule. I would drive home and make a food and exercise plan. Every day I would check SBC. Pictures of St Vincent and Fowler would go on my walls. Until my own photo shoot: no beer, no chocolate, no bread. I would exercise at least once every day. Only black coffees. No food after 8 pm. Scales every morning and night. Aurelius wrote: 'Your mind will be like its habitual thoughts; for the soul becomes dyed with the colour of its thoughts.' My soul would no longer be dyed with the colours of laziness and indulgence and mediocrity.

•

A WEEK INTO the new regime and with no discernible results, I was feeling down about myself so I bought a small book called *Introducing Self-Esteem: A Practical Guide* by David Bonham-Carter. It was about the same dimensions as my mobile phone and had a section for notes in the back. 'FEEL BETTER and worry less,' said the blurb, 'VALUE YOURSELF and over-come feelings of inadequacy'. There were just two pages dedicated to 'accepting your physical appearance'. David mustn't have thought the body was much of a battlefront for self-worth.

'If some of your negative feelings about your-self relate to your appearance, then you can try an exercise involving looking in a full-length mirror and honestly focusing on each of the

17

"bad" aspects of your body that you dislike, but trying to do so in a detached observational way rather than in an emotional self-condemnatory way.' This was called 'detached self-observation' and involved calmness and acceptance. I was to imagine what someone else—an objective third party—would say. When I saw that body in the mirror I was allowed to have self-improvement-style thoughts about it, but I was not to speak about it negatively. Something didn't add up. How could you want to improve something without first acknowledging it required improvement?

For a very long time we hadn't had a full-length mirror in the house, so I bought one from Kmart. I took my shirt off and dropped it on the floor, kicked my undies down my legs and flicked them aside with a twist of my ankle. All my muscles and joints had the ease of movement most 26-year-olds take for granted. I looked into the mirror and my stomach clenched. I saw and

I immediately catalogued: the parts of my thighs that came out further than my hips; the love handles; the formless jelly of the inner thigh; the soft excess at my underarm; the roll between my belly button and pubic line. Worst of all, the scars on my pale thigh from when I used to cut myself and make lists of all the things wrong with me, including that I was fat. It had been ten years since high school, and I was even bigger now than I was when I'd started cutting. What did it all mean? I took a deep breath and tried to start the exercise again.

'You are tall,' I said aloud. It was true.

What else?

'You are pale and have freckles. Your hair is long.'

Then I got stuck. One cannot observe anything without a reference point. Should I say, 'I come in at the waist,' or, 'I go out at the belly'? Both were true. I was tall compared to other women but not to other adult human

19

bodies in Australia. Did I make assessments based on comparisons from when I was lighter or heavier? The body in the mirror existed in the same world as all the 'befores' and 'afters' of eleven seasons of *The Biggest Loser* in Australia alone. I was supposed to focus on the parts that I personally disliked about my body in a calm, accepting, detached way, but if I was calm and accepting I wouldn't have had any parts to look at in the first place and my heart wouldn't have been beating so hard I could see it thumping away under my naked skin.

•

WILL STORR'S BOOK *Selfie* is about America's journey to neoliberalism and the hugely flawed and damaging self-esteem 'movement' of the 1980s. He set out to understand why people became so self-obsessed, and what it was doing both to individuals and to his country. Storr's two stages of considering the 'self' explained why I could have lower weight-related self-esteem than a person with significantly more body fat than me. Not only are we not all inclined towards the 'perfectionist' tendencies that inevitably lead to feeling disappointed, but each of us also has a different definition of what that 'perfection' looks like. Storr went on to explain that you can't just hijack or 'hack' your self-esteem. It's not really possible to improve self-esteem without giving people a reason to feel better about themselves. If your weight is the thing keeping your self-esteem low, then, presuming you have these 'perfectionist' tendencies I like to call 'striving', you have the following options:

1. Match the goal. (Lose weight.)
2. Match the weight. (Change the goal.)

When I considered those two options my stomach sank. I knew how hard it would be to get thin, but the prospect of self-acceptance—resulting in laziness and, therefore, weight gain—made me panic. Option 2 wasn't an option at all.

I put the book down and made a new pact with myself, this time on paper, to try harder. I listed methods, weigh-ins, tips and tricks I found online that sounded cruel enough to be effective. It was a game of the mind; a challenge for the brain that would see the body benefit. When I was running and thought it was hard, I would remind myself that I had to enjoy the stitches for it to work. When I was hungry I would remind myself that I had to enjoy the hunger for it to work. I was allowed an infinite amount of the same food my guinea pigs ate: celery, capsicum and carrot. I turned on push notifications for Instagram accounts that contained supermodels exercising: SBC, Georgia Fowler, Victoria's Secret, and the rest. I would define what my perfect body looked like, I had two months to achieve it, and that would be the body in the photographs. I had the willpower to make it so.

•

IN THE MEANTIME, there was to be an interim photo shoot for a major newspaper's lifestyle lift-out, with the images of me running along-side the first extract of my book to be published anywhere. I was told it would be a big deal. After two weeks, my food diary entries—intended to record kilojoule intake and exercise output—had quickly ballooned to actual diary entries, ruminating on self-discipline like a teenage fan of Aurelius. The push notifications were working well. Being forced to frequently and unpredictably acknowledge that other people were doing better than me at any given moment of any day was a powerful way to obliterate any sense of separation from that parallel universe. The first thing I thought about every day, and the

23

last thing I thought about every night, was what I was striving for.

One Friday I weighed in at 63 kilograms, ran 6 kilometres and ate only lean foods all day. But that night I was so tired, and still so hungry even after eating all my soup, that I had four squares of chocolate. As I tried to get to sleep I berated myself for such a pathetic lapse of control. Unable to switch off, I watched some SBC videos in bed and felt ashamed I couldn't be as strong as those women with their ab lines and silky ponytails. I'd tried to write during the day but had felt headachey and distracted. I wanted to be lean and in control, to fit all my clothes and not think about food all the time. I wanted to be full without food, to transcend it. 'Elevation of the intellect above the workings of the flesh,' Aurelius wrote. My body had to represent my determination.

I was approaching thinness the way one would a mystery: I was trying to solve it, to get to the bottom of it so that I might move on from it. As I got thinner, it was as though I'd picked up a scent, was coming closer to the truth, becoming frenzied in my dedication to the pursuit, rib demanding more rib; both rabid and ravenous.

The day before the shoot for the lift-out I paid $120 for a haircut and blow-dry and felt elated when I fit into a pair of pants I used to wear when I was at university. But then I cried in the car going home from the hairdresser's; all that money I'd spent on my hair was wasted because I was still stuck with the same fugly face and huge body. I felt embarrassed for even trying to be beautiful.

In the days that followed I ran further and faster, and ate less and less. When I saw the photos from that shoot in a mock-up of the article, I looked like my normal self, not skinny the way I wanted. What I wanted was Joan Didion leaning on her Corvette Stingray. The

25

editors of the magazine had taken my book and butchered it. They chopped it up and got me to bolt its most salacious, private, traumatic sections back together like I was Dr Frankenstein, and they had rewritten sentences of their own choosing, deleted others, and changed the final line. I was to fill the gaps with excruciatingly revealing, exposing information, in as few words as possible.

Two days later I was sent a new mock-up of the article to fit the edits and discovered they had used a different image of me. In the new photo I was a much smaller figure within the frame, so far away you couldn't even see my figure. All the effort I'd gone to so far had been pointless.

On the day when I insisted the final line of the 'excerpt' be the one I actually wrote myself, I had gone for a long run and eaten only a carrot salad and drunk some black coffees. When a powerful migraine hit me at 6 pm I had to call my boyfriend to collect me from work.

In the car I burst into tears. 'It hurts,' I wept.

'Is it just the migraine?' he asked gently. 'You're not upset about anything else?'

'No,' I lied.

The next morning, still wobbly on my legs, I stepped onto the scales and was met with a blinking 62 kilograms, and euphoria rushed through me, determination renewed, a triumph. A hard run, only coffees, much stress, one light meal, then migraine and bed. That's how I would see progress. The photo shoot—the big one—would take place in Sydney in two weeks. I went to the kitchen to make myself a coffee and popped more painkillers. Would it cost me my physical health to get down to 60 kilos? Undoubtedly. So what? I could just get the good photo and then relax, right? Easy, done. But what if there were more photos after that? What if I went on television one day? What if it didn't

27

stop? I watched the kettle boil, steam rising from the plastic mouth until the pressure was high enough to switch the whole thing off.

•

THE INWARD FOCUS intensified. I stretched out on the bed, cat-like, and rapped my knuckles against my ribs, admiring how in the afternoon sun each one struck a shadow on my skin. When I got hungry and felt my resolve failing, I would simply scroll through endless pages of online clothing stores or buy lots of new beauty products. There was an advertisement on television for a product called 'Thin Lizzy'. It looked cheap, with bad graphic design, low production quality, and a 'buy one get one free' offer. I couldn't understand the 'Thin' part of the brand name until I saw that their logo featured the silhouette of a thin woman. Presumably, that was Lizzy. The foundation was thick and went on quick. A young woman who had a birthmark on her chin talked about how she'd struggled to be self-confident, but with Thin Lizzy on her face she could go out into the world finally feeling like herself. 'You can show everyone who you truly are,' the voiceover said, as 'before' and 'after' pictures flashed up on the screen. This woman had to cover her face to show us what she felt was truly underneath.

I went to Mecca Maxima, a beauty store, and having convinced myself that 'clear skin' and 'shiny hair' weren't 'fake' or 'vapid' like a full face of make-up was, spent almost $300 on serums and oils to get rid of pores and acne scars. Some of the products were named after their dermatologist creators, differentiating themselves from the Kardashian-named lipsticks that came in bold and often unnatural colours. I was just trying to show people my real, clean face. The best version of me had 'glowing, fresh skin'. The real me may have had acne, but the real me didn't identify with having had acne,

29

and a scar-free face would be a more accurate representation of the person I determined myself to be.

I left the quiet aisles, having touched rare waters to my fingers and face, wondering at the promise of that land. I liked going in there, but not in my daggy clothes with unwashed hair. It was similar to SBC only allowing already-thin women to take their exercise classes. I enjoyed going into Mecca stores in the same way I enjoyed the swanning you do when you're all dressed up and walking from dinner to the theatre; there is something good about the richness of it all. I took the richness from the luxurious shelves at Mecca, and I acquired it with my richness, and at home I put this richness on my face, and it helped to further reveal my richness. When I worked hard and made more money and spent it there, it would help me grow more beautiful, and everyone would be able to see it. In the store, the attentiveness of the woman with the black apron was flattering and reassuring. She had guided me through the products. I had suspended my disbelief to gloss over the fact that she was paid to be there, and so her gaze and the altered octave of her voice were still affirming. What was that attention a surrogate for? A lover's? A servant's? For whom did I want to be beautiful? For Mecca itself, perhaps? To look better each time I went in, to be one of its people?

Perhaps I was the tenant secretly aspiring to landlord status, to one day set the rules instead of following them. Except it got harder every day you got older—which was every day—to follow those rules. And to get close enough to the top, to the place from which the commandments descended, how could I? Who even sat in the clouds setting the rules now? The models simply enacted them; they were the signal boost not the source of the message. The ironically faceless advertisers told us which faces to chase, but why did we let them if not out of fear of each other and a pressure from all around? At the checkout the aproned woman congratulated me on reaching the second tier of their loyalty program, indicating how many hundreds of dollars I'd spent there within the last twelve months.

'Do I look like I spend that much money here?' I wanted to ask. 'Does it show? Is it working yet?'

•

IN 2016 HAYDEN LaFever, a master's student from Middle Tennessee State University, presented his thesis titled 'The Effects of 3D Body Representation and Somatomorphic Images on Self-Esteem'. In the course of his research, he'd found that people did not appreciate being confronted with exact 3D replicas of what their bodies looked like. I laughed when I read the extract. The results showed a clear and immediate plummeting of self-esteem when people were shown their scans. This was despite most of the participants presumably having looked at themselves in the mirror that day, or at least once that week. This was despite those participants knowing, when they did up their belts or pulled up the zippers on their dresses, that they could or could not fit into their clothes. Something about being truly detached from the body they were observing confronted them with the reality of their size. Maybe we know but don't like thinking about it, so pretend not to know? If so, what are we seeing when we look at ourselves in the mirror? For people with eating disorders, 'body dysmorphia' is the term for the discrepancy between what they see in the mirror and what they really look like. In contrast to the participants in LaFever's study, an anorexic or bulimic person with body dysmorphia sees themselves as bigger than they actually are, which raises the question: would their self-esteem skyrocket if they were presented with a

33

3D model of themselves? Unlikely. They're in that two-minus-two-minus-two-until-you-get-to-zero headspace. I was there once and that's how I got down to 57 kilograms and that was when I thought I was the most beautiful version of Bri and the rest of the world did too. We are incapable of seeing ourselves clearly.

The term 'body image' was first defined in 1935 by psychiatrist Paul Schilder, a pupil of Sigmund Freud, as 'a person's perception of the aesthetics or sexual attractiveness of their own body'. In her 2018 book *The Psychology of Fashion*, Carolyn Mair explains how the body has come to be considered a 'signifier' of the individual, because of all the choices we can make about culture, belonging, social relations and personal activities. For example, studies repeatedly demonstrate that 'feeling well-dressed' leads to greater feelings of 'sociability, power, and worth'. I chewed on that idea, that sense, of 'worth'. Why did some people feel they were worth more than others? Why did some people commit acts against others that clearly indicated they thought their *wants* were worth more than someone else's *needs*, like safety? How could I interact with people in a way that told them I thought they were worthwhile? Was it possible for me to think I was worth less, sometimes even worthless, when I was big, and was it possible for me to harbour those thoughts without ever implicitly or explicitly communicating them to the world around me?

•

ONE WEEK LATER I hit 61 kilograms. Closing in for the kill, I went shopping for jeans, knowing what a painful process it would be, hoping it would force me to confront how much progress still lay ahead. Knowing that when I looked in the mirror I could not truly see myself, I took photos of myself in each pair—front, side, behind—then I sat in the chair of the change

35

room and flicked through the images side by side. I hated them all.

'Jeans are the worst,' the attendant said sweetly on the other side of the change-room door. 'It's so hard to find ones you feel comfortable in.'

I thought about her comment on my way to a different store. It was untrue. In fact, finding comfortable jeans would be easy. She didn't mean comfortable jeans; she meant jeans in which you felt comfortable within yourself because of how you looked to other people.

At the second store I asked for a smaller size and a tighter pair, and I bought them. They had some diagonal stitching on the front, and they were so tight that when I took them off there were red diagonal lines imprinted on my skin. There was a message there—the lines ran over the top of my long-ago self-harm scars— but I failed to read it. When I stepped out of the change room I felt like a great success.

That afternoon I posted a picture of myself wearing them on Instagram, and the likes and comments rolled in. My eyes lit up with the reflection of the scrolling screen, my brain lit up like a dopamine laser show. It was almost time to launch the book. My image, my body, my photographs—it was all part of my work, my identity.

•

ONE NIGHT IN May I went out with friends to a new brewery. It was a cool industrial space, with the tanks on display, polished concrete floors, high ceilings and dogs allowed. They only served beer and pizza.

'Great!' I said and acted normal, ordering two pints of beer and a margherita. But I felt extremely anxious when I went to bed later that night.

'I can feel it in my belly,' I said to my boyfriend in the dark.

'Of course you can, it's wonderful,' he replied and drifted off.

I feared the very fullness he cherished, and I would not be able to take the thinness much further without upsetting my social life. I lay in bed, trying to sleep, but in my mind I saw slow-motion clips of me shoving food into my mouth, a grotesque close-up of dribble sliding down my chin, chocolate caught under my dirty finger-nails. How could I ever amount to anything if I couldn't even control myself in this, the most simple human endeavour?

The next day I ate nothing but two light Cruskits and three mini pieces of sushi. When I thought about how I was surviving—still running and working and travelling—on such a small amount of food, I thought back to previous times in my life when I would eat three meals each day plus snacks, and I wondered if that was gluttonous of me, and if some shame came from that excess consumption. But my squandering manifested in all things. I drove a car too much and I bought too many disposable objects, and I didn't feel real shame about any of that waste. It was not the indulgence itself that was the problem. Would starving myself always feel like a battle and a failure unless, or until, it killed me? Only then would I know I'd pushed myself as far as I could. Only then could I be sure I'd done my best, perfected the pursuit: when I watched my family crying at a hospital bed through slits beneath my tired eyelids. I loathed that image and absolutely did not want that kind of attention. It transported me back to the newsagent's and the longing for invisibility—or, more accurately, really, for people to see past my body. What could I have pinned on my chest to take the place of a jutting clavicle? A could-if-I-wanted-to medal? Proof for myself and anyone looking that I was capable of anything I set my mind to. That I dreamed of a self more grand than

39

my corporeal trappings; that I was not afraid of spending a lifetime pursuing perfection for either my self or my work.

Two days and much exercise later, I stepped on the scales, and the numbers blinked back at me: 60.5 kilograms. I'd hit it: the six-zero mark. Another two days and it could be 60.0—or even a touch lower—in time for my trip to Sydney and the big photo shoot. I was at the gates of the promised land, but what gripped me was fear. Immediate and intense fear. One day I would get big again. I couldn't be happy about thinness knowing I was sacrificing a future self who might one day return to a rounder figure. You can't be happy about good reviews of your book if you're not then sad, hurt, and offended by the bad ones. If I wanted to truly know myself, I could not just pick and choose when I let the opinions of others affect my self-perception.

I looked in the mirror. My face had changed, I was sure of it; it was more angular. I liked it.

Outside on the deck of my unit cigarette ash caught on my forearm hair before I realised I was smoking again. The models had the real drugs, I should at least get the cigarettes. It had been a while, so two in a row made me feel sick. 'Good,' I said aloud to nobody else, stubbing the butt into the heel of my shoe, leaning on the rail to steady myself as I stood up again.

•

I READ IN *The New Yorker* that the French impressionist Chaim Soutine, one of my favourite painters, would often skip meals to save money for art supplies. That was an aspiration of mine. To put practice before indulgence and take the art higher somehow. Aurelius knew it too. Of craftsmen he said, 'These men, when their heart is in it, are ready to sacrifice food and sleep to the advancement of their chosen pursuit.' But then Soutine would also throw brushes away instead of cleaning them. What was up with

41

that? He mustn't have found food to be that much of a sacrifice. I thought it was a sacrifice. All my life, whenever I was down or exhausted, a bowl of spaghetti could be like a blood transfusion. Cooking took me out of myself the same way playing with animals did. Even as a child I loved the stimulation and distraction of grocery shopping. I still feel that on a scorching day an icy lemon drink is like a small, tangy gift from Summer herself.

I thought of Soutine when I watched the documentary *Dries* in an absolute rapture. The designer's singular, meticulous focus is awe-inspiring. The people near him seem to mould their lives not around him, but around his work. Somehow his eyes are always directed forward, always noticing and absorbing information, so that it would be silly to pay attention to him instead of what he is doing and where he is looking. He becomes a conduit then for their efforts as well as his own. His gentle physicality offsets what otherwise could be described as a forceful presence. After decades of hard work, he's now able to enjoy certain luxuries, but this doesn't seem to cloud his creativity or productivity. He is a creative genius. I revere him, I adore what he makes, and I long to know him better. I yearn to emulate this steadfast dedication, this true and pure *love* he has for the work itself.

But the film is also full of models. Naturally, as a fashion designer, he works with models, but his are thin-thin. He is high fashion, and the higher the fashion, the more the joints must protrude. One of the most damaging models on the catwalk while I was in high school was the Australian Gemma Ward, who has only recently started speaking about her extreme thinness as being 'pretty scary'. When I was in year ten, in 2006, Ward walked for Dries. My hand paused, hovering over my small serve of popcorn, longing to be a part of the Dries world as I felt a fissure within me grow. Sitting

43

in the cinema, I watched Dries watching the models on his runway at the big, climactic show scene. Did I want to be the model, or did I want to be Dries? I could not be both. The perfect body wore his clothes while he himself seemed to maintain a regular diet and enjoy cooking. The models' legs were like over-pulled toffee, stretched so thin and brittle it was a miracle they didn't snap. And who did I want this perfection *for*? There was something so tempting about the way the models were gazed upon and admired, but probably none of them would ever have a documentary made about their vision and craft. Thirty models, but only one Dries. When the crowd clapped at the end of the show it was for the garment not the coathanger.

Interviewed by Hanya Yanagihara for *T Magazine*, Dries said about his famously beautiful and well-tended garden (which featured prominently in the documentary): 'You plan and plan, and something always goes awry anyway. The depressed gardener knows that. He also knows, however, that it is simply what happens when you try to control what cannot be controlled—to be a depressed gardener is to live in a state of constant humility. But it also means a heightened ability to appreciate the strange gifts that circumstance sometimes affords.' It is Aurelius to my ears. The stoicism is that fundamental acceptance of the volatility of life, and the acknowledgement that to be in the right place at a blossoming moment requires a never-ceasing commitment to craft.

Leaving the cinema it occurred to me that I had been trundling like a toddler down the catwalk following the models in the bright lights instead of quietly slipping behind the curtain backstage to where the real genius was at work. Suddenly social media seemed like a bawdy, vaudevillian shrine to self-involvement. I wasn't sure I could be that perfect artist, though, and I was afraid that if I really tried I would feel as false as I did starving myself. I could never get close to the genius of Soutine or Dries, and so I was back to the beginning again. I could not be that type of perfect, but did not know what was *my* perfect, and if it was possible or even desirable.

•

EGGSHELL SKULL WAS published at the start of June, and when the book tour began it was heaven and hell. I cried in front of crowds as I talked about what I'd survived, and the messages started pouring in. My inbox was screaming at me to read and reply to people's outpourings of pain. In the signing line I was asked for advice, unloaded on, praised, and questioned. There was minimal sleep, maximum drinking, and a growing feeling of being permanently on display. More than ever before my work and my appearance felt inextricably connected. Critically, what I thought would be two weeks of intensity turned

46

into about three months. I was not prepared for the book to do well. Once, a hotel I was staying in asked if they could repost a selfie I took in my room, and I thought that was strange, until I went onto their Instagram feed and saw it was just photos of the hotel interspersed with highly edited pictures of young women. I gave my permission because they had given me a complimentary upgrade, but it made me uneasy to see my face used for their business. I didn't know where to draw the line in using my image, but I could feel my own behaviour contributing to people's attitudes towards the importance of my appearance. Every morning I would put on a full face of make-up, resenting the time it took, but then feel incredibly buoyed to see my social media accounts lighting up and launch events selling out. Zadie Smith said she was becoming frustrated with how long her seven-year-old daughter was spending getting ready, and limited her time in front of the mirror to fifteen minutes each day because anything more was a waste. On an intellectual level I agreed, but it felt like an impossibility for me. I was too afraid of both my book and my body not being good enough.

•

IN *THE PSYCHOLOGY of Fashion* Carolyn Mair explained why the ultra-skinny model is still the ideal in fashion. 'Rapid advances in technology in the 1990s meant we were seeing more images and video footage of designers, models and fashion in general', and the 'heroin-chic' look happened to be 'in' at the time. It has been the hardest ideal to shake because for so much of the world it was the first and most impactful vision of 'style' and 'fashion' they experienced. And it sold well, too, because it was an unattainable and therefore perfect ideal for advertisers to keep pushing. The cruel joke of high fashion houses like Dior and Chanel is that they make most of their money selling accessories and beauty products. Nobody buys the actual clothes they are famous for because once we've seen the straps and swatches on a lithe creature, we cannot stand seeing them on our own lumps and bumps. But a handbag, a pair of shoes, a bottle of perfume or some earrings—these things can fit.

Advertising works by making us feel bad about ourselves, and offering to solve that with purchases. One answer, rather than asking advertisers to change, it is to stop buying their goods until they get the message. But I cannot do this. I love Dries and want to enjoy his clothes without somehow encouraging his encouragement of thinness. And besides, Dries does not even advertise or engage influencers.

Put your own oxygen mask on before helping others to do the same, I heard about twenty times on plane trips once I was on tour. I couldn't fix the system while I myself was so broken. Only

49

once you have oxygen can you think strategic-
ally enough to get off the fucking plane.

I used to watch Victoria's Secret shows when
I was in my early twenties. They get some of
the best performers—Rihanna, Taylor Swift,
Kanye West, Justin Bieber—and it's all perfect.
I'd put the show on and clean my room, or have
it playing while I searched for new lean recipes.
I wanted that body for myself so, so badly. Once,
though, in a cafe in New York, I sat two tables
away from a Victoria's Secret model. We were
both in the cafe for over an hour, but while I
ate some eggs for breakfast all she ordered was
hot water and lemon. How are you supposed
to finish law school if you're just ordering hot
water and lemon? How are you supposed to be
a rock star or a venture capitalist *and* have the
body of the model they date? We follow fashion,
Mair argued, because: 'Imitation affords effortless belonging.' The exercise and diet regime
isn't the 'effortless' part, of course. What Mair

was talking about is our terror at the prospect of having to define success and worth for ourselves individually. 'Evidence shows that a range of biological, psychological and physical risk factors, including body dissatisfaction, perfectionism, genetics, puberty and environmental factors, put individuals at risk for disordered eating.' There is a direct relationship between watching more television and having lower levels of appearance satisfaction. 'The slender, or even thin, ideal is currently considered an essential component of beauty, success, health and control over one's life. Internalisation of the thin ideal predicts increased body dissatisfaction, which can lead to dieting and eating disorders. However, the degree to which individuals are affected by these pressures depends on whether or not they are internalised.' The ideal comes from everything around you, but Aurelius was right: these things can only hurt you if you take them within yourself. 'If you are distressed by anything external, the pain is not due to the thing itself but to your own estimate of it; and this you have the power to revoke at any moment.'

•

THE BIG MAGAZINE shoot was exactly as glamorous as I imagined. The setting was a huge, loft-style space with high walls of windows and white concrete floors. There were tables of make-up and accessories, and they were playing good music. Someone got me a coffee, and I sat sipping it while getting my hair and nails done simultaneously. When it came time to duck behind a screen with the stylist—to try on different outfits by the designer I'd requested—I was confident and happy. Emerging in one outfit to cooing, I changed into another, and was again attended to by make-up artists. I guessed it was how most women want to feel on their wedding day: luxurious and expensive and the centre of attention.

The photographer was chatty and nice, and we moved to a few different spots in the space. On the floor sitting down, leaning against a wall, standing in front of a plinth on which I rested my arms. Each time we moved, four or five men would surround us and shift the screens and lights and bits and bobs. I marvelled at how many people were being paid in that room.

As the hairdresser swooped in to respray and move a stray strand, my publicist called out to me, 'Do you want to go on TV this afternoon? It's Julia Baird from *The Drum* on the phone.'

I looked back at the photographer and grinned, right down the barrel of the lens.

'Yes, that's it, gorgeous,' he said warmly, 'I love that beautiful big smile', and I believed that I was gorgeous and my smile was beautiful, because about a dozen different people had just been paid to render me so. I was being

53

photographed for a glossy magazine and that night would be live on national television, and I was so damn slim. All the hard work was worth it to feel like I deserved to be in that room. To go out into the world talking about surviving being molested as a child without feeling like a complete piece of shit, and to earn a place at tables where conversations on legislation and policy were happening, I had to be the best possible version of me, and that afternoon I truly felt I was.

•

BACK HOME AFTER the photo shoot and the first part of the book tour I read *Selfie* properly and must have been coming back down to earth because it hit me in the gut. Storr documented his own perfectionist tendencies and I saw a lot of myself in his struggle through self-loathing. 'I seem to be caught in a lifelong rhythm of expecting more from myself than my talent and character can supply,' he wrote, and my chest ached with the same timbre of inevitable longing and disappointment reverberating through it. On control, perfectionism, and eating habits, he found that: 'When people are having perfectionist thoughts, they're wanting to feel that they're in control of their mission of being the great person they imagine they ought to be.' When we fail, as we inevitably do, the despair and self-loathing set in. Perfectionism is a significant predictor of disordered eating; Storr noted that, in Britain, 'hospital admissions for eating disorders in young women and girls jumped by 172 per cent in the decade to 2014'.

Social science professor Gordon Flett explained the different types of perfectionism to Storr: social, narcissistic, self-oriented and neurotic. Social perfectionists feel that they are failing to live up to a perfect idea others have of them or put on them. Neurotic perfectionists suffer from low self-esteem and 'just feel like they never measure up'. They're worried and anxious people who experience a 'massive discrepancy' between who they are and who they want to be. They make sweeping generalisations about themselves, so if they're 'not efficient' at a particular thing, they experience it as a failure of the entire self. It can also be conceptualised as slices of a pie—you can dedicate a huge slice of your personal pie to beauty, or a small slice. Regardless of the size of the slices, if you're not careful, a perceived failure in one area can have an overriding effect on the others. Your 'universal' self-esteem is how you feel about yourself altogether. I had been letting one small slice of my pie—my weight—poison the whole thing.

A self-oriented perfectionist experiences demands that perfection 'come from within the self'. At first I thought, 'Ah, that's me', but I also felt a little of each of the others. Pressure from outside like the socials, and a spoiling of the whole pie like the neurotics. Even narcissistic perfectionism—'in which people believe they're absolutely capable of reaching the highest heights, but become vulnerable when they finally realise that, actually, they're not'—is a confronting definition for me.

It is reassuring to read that Storr came to understand that perfectionism isn't so much something you do or do not have, but a pattern of thinking: everyone sits somewhere on the perfectionist scale. We have all, at some point in time, experienced the disappointment of missing a mark. 'That resonant moment of longing sorrow when you realise you've failed—that's what we're talking about.'

Flett and his colleagues are now studying 'perfectionism presentation', which can be exemplified by mine and many people's relationships to their Instagram accounts. I must not only practise perfection but also present it. Then, when I present an image of perfection, I am trapping myself in a feedback loop of having a new goal I need to live up to. Storr presented the shocking statistics of anxiety and disillusionment in modern Western society, along with the observation: 'People are suffering and dying under the torture of the fantasy self they're failing to become.'

This idea of a 'fantasy self' gripped me. I could picture her so vividly. Clear skin, less than 60 kilos, shiny hair, smiling, energetic, easygoing yet high-achieving. Who didn't have a number in their head, and the smiling face of a celebrity or model they took with them to the hairdresser?

Storr started a different section of the book by admitting he struggled with some excess weight in his belly area. 'The lardy bib I keep beneath my shirt is not so much a body part as it is a psychological flaw that's become material—shame I can touch. My fatness, the outline of the body, can make me feel as if I'm guilty of a moral transgression.' Then we learn of *kalok-agathia*, the ancient Greek words for 'beauty' and 'good' mashed together to create a term indicating that beautiful people are good. It's an example of what is often referred to as the 'halo effect', by which our first impressions of people influence our judgement of their character and capability. In *How We Eat With Our Eyes and Think With Our Stomachs: The hidden influences that shape your eating habits*, Melanie Mühl and Diana von Kopp explained that the concept was first introduced by the American psychologist Edward Lee Thorndike. 'During the First World War, Thorndike researched how command personnel assessed their subordinate soldiers. He asked officers for an assessment of the soldiers' physique, character, leadership qualities, and intellect. Soldiers with an attractive face and ideal posture were consistently rated higher than their less physically endearing colleagues.' You can see it in every Disney film where the

59

goodie is beautiful and the baddie is ugly. In blockbusters, too—every Bond villain has a disfigurement of some kind, and in rom-coms the handsome protagonist's 'comedic' sidekick, who is the butt of every joke, is nearly always overweight. In practice it means when we see a person's weight, if we do not approve of it, we automatically presume it represents a failing of their entire self. We don't give them the opportunity to cut their own pies.

Just add social media to that mix and you have a dangerously cruel cocktail of inescapable social pressure and a complete inability to compartmentalise your life. 'Social media is about more than just appearance,' Storr wrote. 'It's also a deeply neoliberal product that has gamified the self, turning our identity into a pawn that plays competitively on digital platforms for likes, feedback, and friends.' While I wasn't necessarily looking for friends, the gamification of my self was very real, and growing.

The more followers I gained as a freelancer, the more likely I was to get writing assignments and speaking gigs. The more pictures I posted of myself in make-up and cool clothes on Instagram, the more followers I got. My boyfriend used to make fun of my selfie-taking antics until we got invited to the glamorous opening night of a new gin bar in town with a three-course snack meal and unlimited cocktails. In the gig economy, a person's social media presence is a potentially lucrative but constantly hungry content-eating monster. Among my generation of feminists we scoff at the prospect of women 'competing' with one another, but anything gamified necessarily has winners and losers. Except perfection and absolute 'beauty' can never truly be attained, and so we render ourselves all just different levels of losers. Even people in salaried positions are under pressure to positively represent the company on their digital platforms, and for women, who are under

61

an aesthetic microscope more often than men, 'positively' means 'good-looking'.

Storr also pointed out that, as we've known about traditional advertising for a long time, 'awareness of the artifice that's inherent in social media is, apparently, no protection'. It's not enough to tell people an image of a model is photoshopped and airbrushed—once the ideal of perfection has been presented to them, it's incredibly difficult to truly reject it or to protect the real, flawed self from trying, and failing, to measure up.

Social media has democratised fashion in a big way. Street style is overtaking the runway, and influencers are being paid more for shoots than professional photographers are for work in magazines. That world, once an elite and distant oligarchy, is real now, and if it's relatable, that means it's *achievable*. It was damaging to compare my body to Georgia Fowler, sure, but what's worse is the other 1500 non-model women in my feed who all look better than me all the time, and I can't tell whether or not they're using filters or beautifying apps. 'One of the dictums that defines our culture is that we can be anything we want to be,' Storr wrote, 'we just have to dream, to put our minds to it, to want it badly enough.' I was waiting to see the photo of myself, wondering if I'd worked hard enough and wanted it badly enough. But they wouldn't let me see it before a hundred thousand other people did.

•

THE MAGAZINE CAME out. The image shocked me.

'I look twelve!' I exclaimed to my publicist.

'You look beautiful,' she insisted, as though it were a rebuttal.

'A beautiful twelve-year-old.'

Wearing barely any make-up, a chubby-cheeked, freckle-faced girl stared back at me. Having been primed and ready to loathe my

63

body, instead I could only really see a face. A face and big tumbling of hair—the close crop meant all that was visible of my body was my forearms and hands. All that hunger had been a waste. I sat down by myself and thought about what I'd wanted and why I didn't feel good. It just wasn't perfect. I'd wanted something commanding, arresting, maybe even dire: a real likeness that captured the striving, wrangling me.

Getting over myself and turning the pages to see the other women featured, though, women like Sharman Stone and Michelle Law, I got angry at just how fucking stupid it would be if they thought they looked bad because they looked 'fat'. Imagine if the world were deprived of their voices and their genius because they were too preoccupied with diets and gruelling thinness regimes? The full body shot I saw and was most impressed by was of soccer player Samantha Kerr, and she was strong! Hers was

the kind of body Lara Croft really needed to

believably perform all those lifts and jumps she does in the movies.

In the caption underneath my picture listing the designer of the clothes I wore and who had done my hair was the line: 'Bri wears Modern Muse perfume by Estée Lauder.' Something inside me—a little illusion I'd been main-taining—split. Nobody had spritzed me with perfume for that shoot. I have never even smelled Modern Muse. It was only two months prior that I had been feeling awful about not measuring up to the 'Modern Muse' on the cover of that same magazine, and the 'faces' of the perfume were Kendall Jenner and Arizona Muse, who are both spindly-thin. What if the image of me had been a full-body shoot and I looked as gaunt as my goal, either in real life or through Photoshop? Who might be reading it and feeling bad, not realising the fakery of the whole thing, and my own fraudulent beha-viour, walking around talking about women's issues while perpetuating our most common, mundane undoing? All that running, all that hunger, to be the best and most real me, and I had just become a tool. Did any of those models ever use the perfume they marketed? The people in the parallel universe might walk and talk, but they were acting on the set of a fake moon landing; once you've seen the strings you cannot unsee them.

The model and influencer Alexa Chung once said, 'Just because I exist in this shape doesn't mean I'm advocating it', but she was wrong. Models model. Chung, Moss, Fowler and Bündchen all make money encouraging us to build ourselves in their images, and theirs are of elbow and knee joints being wider than the surrounding flesh parts. Entire food groups excluded, exclusive gyms, beauty extruded. This is not at all a problem for those who are naturally that thin. It is undeniably a problem when we look at the thousands of girls and women who die every year trying to match their own image to those they are beaten down with every day. 'Nothing tastes as good as skinny feels,' Kate Moss notoriously said at a party as she declined a canapé. I would be giving talks at schools in the months after my book's release. By existing in my shape and standing in front of them as though I had something to say, I would be advocating not just for the issues on which I spoke, but advocating my own existence as worthy of attention and positive regard. Even among friends I was damaging—refusing 'bad' foods and implicitly endorsing a cruel set of behaviours. In harming myself I was harming others. The jig was up.

•

HEATHER WIDDOWS IS the John Ferguson Professor of Global Ethics at the University of Birmingham. Her book *Perfect Me* is subtitled: *Beauty as an ethical ideal*, and I stumbled across it late one night when I was googling different combinations of words around self-esteem, perfectionism and weight. Widdows spent ten chapters building a framework through which to understand how beauty ideals are formed, why we feel productive and good adhering to them in the short term, how they promise the 'good life' package, and how they are impossible ever to truly attain. Essentially, she made the case that being beautiful—and slimness of some kind is a consistent factor of beauty across almost the entire world—is not just a good thing for a person to be, but that more and more we consider a beautiful person to *be* a good person. Fatness is, therefore, a moral failing. The drive towards physical and presentational betterment is a key component of the perfectionism proliferating in the 21st century. Studies Widdows cited show again and again that women would choose to be thin in preference to almost any other personal wish, and that these desires are irrespective of size. Rather than wanting to be 'thin', what we actually want is to be 'thinner'.

Most compelling of all was Widdows' articulation of the idea of the dual self. I know I have my current body, in which my sense of self exists, but I also identify forcefully with an aspirational, imagined self. The more I think of this second, potential self, the more I identify with it and work towards it. Doing so feels good, because I am committing to myself and working towards a goal, but it is not for my body right now; working towards the aspirational self with the kind of commitment I had been showing necessitated a disdain-borderline-revulsion for my actual present self. I find pictures of me trying on jeans confronting, and those people in that study found the true 3D scans of themselves confronting, because we often picture ourselves the way we *want* to be instead of the way we *are*. Without the language to talk about this duality, I could feel simultaneously optimistic and full of self-loathing: feeling rewarded when relinquishing to the extreme demands of the second self, but thinking all the mixed messages were coming from one place.

When we have a set of values—an ideal, a perfection—we define ourselves and others within it. Daily applications of the ideal taking us towards the second self make for 'good' food and 'good' days. I began using words like 'good' and 'bad' in my food diary for meals and exercise, and the journal rapidly degenerated into a diary of 'goodness' and 'badness' generally. Mühl and von Kopp noted that it is only relatively recently that we find ourselves constantly exposed to images of delicious foods, and thus to be on a diet 'is to permanently resist that temptation and to become a master of self-chastisement'. The chastisement is necessary. 'The willpower of even the most ascetically inclined people will eventually buckle under the pressure of ever-present temptation.'

Aurelius may have recommended rising above bodily urges and functions, but he wasn't being constantly reminded that delicious doughnuts were just an Uber Eats order away or that a new gnocchi place had opened up down the road from him. When I put petrol in my car I am tempted by Mars Bars, and even chip packets are deliberately designed to sound good when opened.

To illustrate how beauty can come to define an individual's entire sense of self, Widdows used the example of a child not cleaning their bedroom. 'While the parent may think the child should tidy their bedroom, failure to do so is not global failure of personality or character, but only a local failure. Such failure does not define the child, it is not a judgment of how valuable she is as a person or indicative of how she should be judged in other contexts.' Yet a recent study Widdows cited found that if the technology was available, 11 per cent of couples in the US would

71

abort a fetus if they knew it held a predisposition to obesity. Mair explained that this fat-shaming is internalised from youth. 'Children as young as 4 years old make preferential choices for slimmer over plumper figures, and 6-year-old children prefer "normal" weight rather than overweight friends. Even at this age, boys are more accepting of overweight children.' While impossible to track accurately, the likelihood is that 'parental influence and comments on their children's appearance and eating patterns' result in girls being under more pressure than boys. 'Girls aged 5 to 8 years reported a lower body esteem and increased body size dissatisfaction after exposure to images of Barbie dolls.' There is this idea that somehow we can hold ourselves to a particular standard but not demand it of others, however, our self-loathing is seeping out the sides of our own containers and our children are bearing the brunt of it. If you think you can fear fatness while raising a child to love their body wherever it naturally lands, you are wrong. If you think you can spend money on age-defying facelifts without it affecting your mother's sense of self, you are wrong. Everything you do communicates your standards and ideals to everyone around you.

In a section titled 'Smooth and Luminous', Widdows explained that whereas we used to need to be beautiful on key occasions like weddings and holidays, the constantly recorded nature of society now means we are always on show. Imagining ourselves and our failings being photographed in almost any context makes this 'camera-ready' demand extensive. Social theorist Foucault's famous description of self-policing by the prisoners in the panopticon—a building designed by philosopher and founder of modern utilitarianism Jeremy Bentham—is relevant here. Imagine a circular gaol arranged around a central guard tower from which all the cells are visible. A prisoner cannot be sure whether or not he is being watched, so he behaves as though he is being watched all the time. Hence he is 'self-policing', meaning he has internalised the sense of being observed.

Until the proliferation of smartphones around 2010, we would only feel conscious of being observed in scenarios that were laden with photo opportunities, but now, with social media being the omnipresent mass-reaching norm, we self-police in perpetuity. Add to that the consideration that social media has made firm what was previously nebulous—quantifiable data outcomes—and you have a dangerous mix of effort and reward. On my book tour I was watched and documented more than ever, and even when I was home in my pyjamas I was seeing comparisons of people doing better and being better than me at all times. This habit of internalised observa-tion does not see or respect the public–private divide; our homes are a permanent open-house inspection. This was Mair's definition of Social Comparison Theory, when 'we are motivated to gain accurate and positive self-evaluations through comparing ourselves to others for self-enhancement'. I can track my progress with followers, likes, and comments, and the halo effect means that how every single other facet of my identity is perceived depends on my appearance being thin, young, and hairless. Even if you try to remind yourself of those old sayings of 'only beating who you were yesterday', you're still going to get stuck in the feedback loop.

What most of us call makeovers and exercise, Widdows referred to as 'body work'. We aim to better ourselves by improving our bodies. 'The body as the focus of effort when it comes to changing and improving the self, rather than the character or the mind, is a recent phenomenon, and without this underpinning assumption the beauty ideal could not be an ethical ideal.' Of course there are real-life health benefits associated with exercising, but the 'body work' principle also applies to small rituals like hair removal, and large commitments like surgery or injections. Hitting the pavement is as much body work as getting lip fillers is, and: 'The more we invest in the transformation, the more we identify with it, the harder we are likely to work.' The more weight I lost, the more I spent on beauty products, new clothes and haircuts. It was like I had held a magnifying glass over this one piece of my pie and revealed all my flaws to myself, and addressing each one made me feel good, because I was bettering myself, so I did it more and more. The hunger for improvement was insatiable and so, when watered, naturally grew. The fact that the beauty ideal is sometimes enjoyable to pursue, and that it brings rewards, and that it always promises the 'good life', makes it extremely difficult to banish this second, aspirational self.

We genuinely think we will be happier if we

look better, and the halo effect proves this is at least partially true. Thinness promises me the feeling I get from Mecca Maxima: the attention, the richness, and the self-confidence. If only I tried hard enough, everyone else could see 'the real me' too. 'The imagined self who looks a certain way is also imagined being a certain way,' Widdows explained, and that imagination runs wild. We are better at work, better in our relationships, better at sex, and basically better at everything in life. In imagining the aspirational self this way, we actively do the whole-pie-spoiling thing to ourselves too. When I imagine myself being more successful when I hit that beauty goal, I am foiling my chances of ever feeling successful in other areas unless or until I do hit that goal. When I picture Joan Didion lounging against the car, I long for both her figure and her talent. I don't just want to be that thin, I want to be that person. When all our images of happiness and success are also skinny, young, and hairless, it becomes a never-fulfilling prophecy.

Widdows pointed out that the only women she had encountered—either through her research or in her own life—who were able to succeed in rejecting and resisting the beauty ideal 'either do so at significant cost and some effort, or they are protected from the costs of nonconformity by membership in a community that endorses some other competing beauty ideal or other ideals that oppose the dominant beauty ideal. These communities are increasingly rare, and often privileged.' Academics were one example she cited. They operate in a well-paid environment where intellectual prowess is held in high esteem, a focus on appearance is considered vain and silly, and a different kind of striving is elevated. What a coincidence, then, that my first book was published to some success, and I started a postgraduate degree, and gradually felt less pressured to adhere to the ideal of beauty and perfection that once kept me awake at night with guilt.

•

IN LATE JULY I was invited to the launch of the magazine and the annual 'Visionary Women' dinner. It was a delightful day and night. I sat in the bar downstairs with martinis and fries, relishing the salt grains grazing the cracks in my chapped lips before the coolness of the martini glass soothed the sting. Then I spent over an hour getting ready. There were huge mirrors, a special UFO-shaped light for make-up application and selfies, and I slipped into the exquisite dress from a not-yet-available collection worth over $1000 that I had been sent for the occasion. At the drinks before the dinner I met the previous editor of a different big magazine and I saw a famous Instagram influencer say 'no, thank you' to canapés. It felt fun and fabulous for about thirty minutes, then I turned to the friend I'd brought as my plus one and said, 'I feel funny.'

She nodded. 'Same.'

At dinner I sat between two fantastically intelligent women in the magazine and art worlds who spent quite some time talking about their horses. At first I scoffed at the luxurious absurdity of their detailed discussion, then I stopped and looked around. The flowers for the centrepieces were already dying. Huge platters of unfinished cheeses were being taken away to be binned. I wasn't even at the big-deal table. One of the magazine's writers showed me a not-yet-released image of an up-and-coming model from a shoot they'd just finished. She had luminous skin, blonde hair and blue eyes, and she was of course very tall and very thin. Then the writer showed me a photo of her daughter mucking around on the set. It was a shock to my system. A physical manifestation of the worlds colliding. *You are doing this to your daugh-ter!* I thought, but didn't say, because the woman was very nice. Everyone was nice. There was a huge photo of each of the Visionary Women on the wall so my twelve-year-old face looked down over all the money. There were two women at our table from the sponsoring cosmetics company. I thought back to the Thin Lizzy ad. There was really no difference between any of the brands, it was just a question of how much money the company had and what audience they were aiming for. Are you a 'Thin Lizzy woman' or an 'Estée Lauder woman'? They both promise to 'reveal the real you' in some way or other. I felt simultaneously celebrated and sold, or sold to.

The editor gave a short speech about how the annual feature, once titled 'Fabulous at Any Age', had been renamed because it was so outdated to put women into age-based categories. Then some of us spoke on a panel about our 'visions' for

81

'empowerment'. Everyone clapped and nodded, but at the end of the night we got gift bags, and in them was age-fighting under-eye anti-wrinkle cream. Back in my room, using three wipes to remove all my make-up, I un-boxed the eye cream from its beautiful packaging. The tiny pot was heavy, with beautiful blue glass and a shiny chrome lid. I wasn't yet battling wrinkles, but this was another reminder that the aspirational self drifts further and further from the ideal self every single day. That was a room full of women talking about lifting each other up, but they all collectively maintained and intensified the standards that trapped them. The perpetuation—the sheer perpetuation of it all—and I was stepping into it, into that already-running river of ideals and perfections. I looked at myself in the UFO mirror. Should I swim against the stream, or step out of the river? Could I?

I READ *PERFECT Me* on the plane home. It made me uncomfortable, not knowing what that dinner meant and what role I had just played. In the face of the relentless march of ageing it doesn't matter how strongly we commit to our second, aspirational selves, since, as Widdows observed, 'Over the long term, inevitably and ultimately, we will fail aesthetically, we will wrinkle and sag, but morally we can succeed at the level of habits and practices, as we keep working on our bodies.' A 40-year-old woman is not a 'bad' person so long as she's trying so hard that she has the legs and face of a 30-year-old. It's not really about young; it's about *younger*.

Foucault's idea of power being exerted from all sides, often internalised, rings true to me. Liberal theory suggests we all make free and voluntary choices all the time, and it struggles to accommodate cultural considerations and the process of internalisation. How do I know if I am a 'self-orientated perfectionist' instead

of a 'social perfectionist' when I have overwhelmingly been raised on the Kool Aid of
slim superiority? Widdows described Foucault's
notion of power as 'diversified, networked, and
creative', and I saw it played out perfectly at the
fancy magazine dinner. The power of the youth-
ful beauty ideal was encouraged by advertisers,
sure, but it was also permitted and perpetuated
by the women in the room and, despite the name
change to 'Visionary Women', by the publication, and by me too. Mair wrote about this
peer-level influence that knowing someone who
had undergone cosmetic surgery significantly
increased interest in having surgery oneself. We
were all swallowing it then regurgitating it to
each other like dumb birds.

Any plan I made had to begin with a sever-
ing of that second, aspirational self, but how to
drive Bri 2.0 out into the desert without feeling
like a complete failure? To remove the potential for an 'after' photo I needed to accept the

'before' photo as the sole source of my self-esteem and identity. That thought was so terrifying I politely declined the flight attendant's offer of a muffin even as my belly rumbled. I was inching closer to an understanding of my own perfectionism, aware that I would slowly kill myself if I didn't kill off that second self. I didn't have to 'let myself go', I just needed to let *that* self go. And that was the answer, really, to my Marcus Aurelius shower dilemma. Bravery is courage in the face of fear; discipline is acting on it. If accepting myself was the best but most daunting prospect, then it was the one I must move towards. The bravery would come in learning how to dress myself, walk and talk, make love, and speak in public in whatever body I had when I stopped hating it. The beast that truly needed beating was the one I imagined, not the one I was.

•

I HAD BEEN going easy on myself for a few weeks when I spent a week as a writer in residence at a smallish, girls-only private school about 30 minutes from Brisbane's CBD. I had been invited there to talk to the students not only about writing, but also about sexual consent. The teachers seemed genuinely relieved to have someone else say what they couldn't; someone who could use words like 'dickhead' and 'bull-shit' and 'sexy' in a way that might actually get through to a thirteen-year-old. In one of the small group writing workshops, I had about a dozen girls from all different year levels prac-tising writing and editing exercises. Part of my job was to make them feel confident enough to share their work and their stories. Two of the older girls were clearly acting too-cool, but there was one girl from the youngest group of students who was delightfully unselfconscious. She asked questions and made comments at the end of each session, was attentive throughout, only occasionally fidgeting due to uncontainable excitement. The exercise involved writing 200 words about how they got from home to school that day, and then we all worked on editing the writing to enhance the exciting parts and strip away the boring parts. When it was time to share, this particular girl rose from her seat and cleared her throat, and with complete earnestness delivered her piece about getting the bus to school.

'When I sat down I looked out the window and wondered what the day had in store for me. Will I eat chocolate? Will I make mistakes?'

The teachers and I burst out laughing.

'You've hit on a universal human truth,' I said. 'You will ask these questions of yourself every day for the rest of your life.'

Later in the afternoon I spoke to the older girls about consent and made sure to include content about sexting as well as physical interactions. There were a lot of questions about nudes at the end that came from victim-blaming, slut-shaming rhetoric, and I was shocked and disappointed. 'But if he didn't even ask for a nude and she sent it, he can do whatever he wants with it, right, because she's just given it up?'

The devaluing of the body was integral to those power dynamics. If we feel even slightly or subconsciously ashamed of parts of our bodies, if they are alien to us and not what we want, it is striking how much more abuse of them we will accept.

In *Woman of Substances*, Jenny Valentish masterfully revealed how little of our understandings of addiction and substance abuse come from women's experiences of either the substances or the systems designed to treat them. I read it the year it came out, 2017, and found it both agonising and revelatory. Most facilities for treating either addiction or disordered eating won't take a woman struggling with both simultaneously. Valentish referred to the 'triumvirate of self-destruct-ive behaviour' being substance abuse, eating disorders, and self-mutilation, and noted, 'The three can often rotate or coexist.' There is so much to unpack here, but what I keep coming back to is a sense of worth and value, or the absence of it, in so many young women. 'The professionals whom I interviewed for this book variously said that around seventy per cent to "ninety-nine-point-nine" per cent of their female clients had been sexually abused as chil-dren.' There is a similarly stark correlation between sexual trauma and both self-harming and disordered eating behaviours. At least one in five women in Australia have been sexu-ally abused as children or sexually assaulted as adults. These crimes are committed almost exclusively by men, and the most at-risk demo-graphic for being targeted is young teenage girls. The acts communicate both explicitly and implicitly that we have less worth than men,

89

and this feeling is amplified by how we are disbelieved and disregarded if we try to speak out against offenders. As Valentish wrote, girls are much 'more likely to beat themselves up than bash somebody else. Any act of aggression against one's own body is also an act of regaining ownership of it, which can be particularly appealing to a woman with little autonomy.' What we put in our bodies and what we do to them is so interconnected with self-esteem and self-value. It feels like the constant diminution of female self-harm and disordered eating— especially these behaviours in teenagers and young women—is some next-level gaslighting. Girls are told their bodies aren't valuable, then people roll their eyes if the girls themselves treat their bodies like trash. How do we still refuse to acknowledge the interconnectedness of all this?

In one of the final writing sessions at the school, we focused on life writing, and a Pacific

Islander girl got up and told a hilarious story about an encounter with a plover. Her mother had always been good with animals, and she presumed she'd inherited that trait until a one-foot-tall bird chased her across a footy field. She was in year nine and her body was bigger— both taller and wider—than any of her peers, who were mostly Caucasian or Asian. What did she think and feel about her body compared to both the thinness *and* the whiteness that was so pervasive? She had such a wicked sense of comedic timing, it was awful to think of how she might be silenced or kept from sharing that voice because what she looked like didn't fit the casting on our screens.

At lunch the long line of excited young bodies jostled in the doorway to the tuckshop, and a teacher led me past them to the front to pick what I wanted to eat. They hushed a bit as they saw me deciding. What did I owe them? What was I saying to them when I wasn't talking?

I was thinking about how many kilojoules were in the 'healthy' option of yoghurt and granola, and how good the cookies looked.

I love watching documentaries about those I admire to learn everything I can about them. I read the books written about them, and I yearn for their greatness, so I do what they do. I certainly wasn't a hero or an idol or anything so extreme, but I had a small part to play in the messages these girls were receiving about the real world that would soon receive them. To ignore or reject that responsibility would be to fail at the delivery of the core message of my entire visit and work: that each of us has equal, inalienable value, and it is right to stand up for it.

•

I FIRST MET Nkechi Anele backstage just before we were going to be on a panel together at Splendour in the Grass. The panel was about women's safety in the music scene, and I was so shocked by the stories Nkechi shared from her time as frontwoman of her band Saskwatch, but more than that I was impressed by how articulate and composed she was in the face of such frustrating and frightening events. She co-created a discussion platform called 'The Pin', which facilitates conversations with multinational and multicultural people about race, identity, and culture within the Australian narrative, and she's also a presenter on triple j.

In the green room after our event, I was waiting for Henry Rollins to arrive because he had liked what I said on the panel opposite him and wanted to chat, and to my delight Nkechi and I had a great conversation over the hour in which he didn't show up. When she asked me what I was working on, I told her I was grappling with the philosophical question: can we have one set of values and rules for ourselves, and another set for others, particularly around

93

our bodies? When Nkechi started talking about her natural hair and how she felt about it for so many years, I was shocked and shattered.

'I would look at my natural hair in the mirror and just think: *you look like a bush bitch.*'

Nkechi is stunning to look at: badass and divine. As I listened to her talk about the years of her struggling to work with and accept her natural hair, I realised that there was an entire language around African women's beauty struggles that I have been deaf to. In an article in *The Guardian*, she said she agreed with a friend who explained to her that 'hair to African women is like weight to white women. It's very important to maintain and it also establishes how you see yourself and how you feel about yourself in society.' I spoke to Nkechi on the phone about this a few months later.

'Hair for me was my huge shame in being black. I love my skin regardless of anything else, but the hair—this monstrosity on my head—and not knowing how to take care of it. I've gone through having my hair braided as a child to chemically straightened as a teenager, then cornrowed . . . only in the last few years before deciding to go natural with the help of my best friend. Even after two years of having my hair out and being very comfortable, I found myself feeling the same fears surface when I had my hair braided again last year, and I was still reluctant to let my afro out in between styles because I didn't want people to perceive me differently. I was ashamed that the real natural me would prevent people from seeing me as human anymore.'

We talked about how for Black women every single hairstyle is a political statement—their entire look is always a statement. They're forced to represent their whole community or culture. An afro is a statement, reminiscent of revolution and the 60s and counterculture. Cornrows are a statement, with so many Europeans only associating the style with hip-hop and criminals. I've interviewed Black women who say that having their hair either braided or natural was seen as 'unprofessional' in corporate environments. Their only options are a straight weave or to have their hair constantly chemically straightened. 'So many successful Black women out there look very put-together,' Nkechi said. 'We're not afforded the space if we're not. Oprah would never be caught dead with natural hair, and if she did it now they'd say she'd gone mad. It would be news like when Britney Spears shaved her head—Black women's hair is so tied up with perceived sanity together-ness and beauty standards.'

I asked her where that term 'bush bitch' came from because the way she said it seemed connected to this language of 'together-ness' or composure, or whatever the opposite was— wildness? She told me about an awful Eddie Murphy show in which he described marrying an African woman and bringing her to the US, 'And the way he spoke about her was as though she was primitive. It's almost like she was a monster. Not a human being, an animal that has gotten away with hanging out with humans. It's unkempt, a monstrous female form pretending to be human. It's also manic. You're not sane, you're crazy, less-than.'

That's what Nkechi used to say to herself in the mirror: bush bitch. And yet, intellectually, she knew how awful this was, and agreed that 'People would be shocked if they heard the way women spoke to themselves.'

I asked her again how there could possibly be such different standards: the ones we hold for ourselves and the ones we hold for others. 'My uncle once told me that there are different types of shame. There is the shame of having done something, and then we are ashamed on behalf of someone else. Most commonly, feeling that we have offended someone else by our presence. Like when you go into a change room, and don't want to make other people see your body. You want to be invisible because you don't want to offend other people with your presence.' I know this feeling. This pre-emptive apology. It comes from the same dank well as the pressure to diet-talk in front of our friends, or preface appearances with apologies for somehow not being up to scratch. We are so incredibly low on self-value as a resource that we feel we are doing wrong by even inflicting our physical presence upon others. Nkechi said the voice inside our heads is the same one we use for regular, non-awful thinking, and so it sounds logical. Often it's not until we are forced to articulate our thoughts—either on paper or aloud to each other—that we can even begin to hear how absurd and cruel we are being.

Thinking of other publicly 'put-together' Black women, I brought up the photo of Ed Sheeran and Beyoncé on stage together for a duet that went viral and spawned hundreds of think pieces on presentational double standards. She's in a giant fuchsia couture gown, with full hair and make-up, and he's in jeans and a t-shirt. We laughed, but Nkechi went on to talk about Beyoncé's Coachella performance, 'When she wore denim jeans and a hoodie to the biggest performance of her life, there was pushback, and that's someone at her level still having to present as an extremely put-together Black woman to be taken seriously. She has to be the extreme of beauty, sanity, creativity, and even then she's not acknowledged for the work she does. And that's the same feeling a lot of Black women have, and it's reinforced in our culture, that you put all this effort in and go above and beyond and yet you're still somehow invisible.'

Of course, it's also not just one or the other: body or hair being judged. The insidiousness of intersectional racism and sexism means that Nkechi's body is judged in a way mine is not, and her hair is judged in a way mine is not, and then the combination of these things is judged in a way I will never have to handle. When I lived in China for a year my heart would sink at the aisles full of skin-whitening creams and lotions I saw in every supermarket. An Australian-born Sri Lankan friend of mine who wanted to be an actress would talk about her older family members deriding her if she got 'too dark' in the sun over the summer. I've never had to grapple with any of this.

'For most women of colour, the struggle is to be seen as a human being,' Nkechi said. 'Especially for African women, we're seen to be too masculine no matter what we do: too aggress-ive, dominant, and hard, and the struggle to seem feminine is the huge battle we go through. It's taken me until 30 to finally lean into it, and now I've started doing weights, and getting strong and athletic.' She's finally arrived—or has begun the process of arriving—at a place where the bad thoughts aren't quite as quick to arrive, or as vicious. 'In the last two years is the first time I've actually felt like I looked beautiful. It means I can actually look myself in the eye when I look in the mirror or be calm in photos. I never felt that before. I used to go into photos thinking I'd ruin them, and think, *How did you get here, how did you get this far?*'

•

IN *THE BEAUTY MYTH*, Naomi Wolf described beauty and dieting products and neuroses as having replaced cleaning products and the trappings of domestic servitude for the modern, educated woman. The book was published the year I was born (almost thirty years ago) but much of it is as fresh as ever. 'The qualities that a given period calls beautiful in women are merely symbols of the female behaviour that that period considers desirable: The beauty myth is always actually prescribing behaviour and not

101

appearance.' It is as Widdows wrote and as I have felt myself: the awful drive is not really to be thin, but because I feel bad if I am not hard at work trying to be thinner.

One of the teachers at the school I visited told me that until the previous principal retired a few years prior, the institutional attitude was like that of a finishing school. The community of teachers and parents were supposed to be proud of teaching the girls deportment and demureness. I pictured the 1950s housewives that Wolf was referring to and wondered about the current equivalent. What does a woman look like when she fulfils all the new pressures that have replaced that straight-backed, smiling domesticity? What's the 2020 version of balancing books on your head while you vacuum? It used to be that keeping the home nice was a huge part of a woman's identity, with motherhood and wifedom the other huge slices of her sense-of-self pie. Now, certainly, career is a bigger aspiration than ever before, but undeniably the rigours of appearance have grown to unprecedented levels. Girls can aspire to be prime minister but are also existing in a state of what Wolf described as 'semistarvation' in order to feel successful—to fit the only image of successful women they're sold. 'Keeping women hungry,' she wrote, is a 'preemptive strike' in keeping them subjugated. A hungry, self-loathing woman cannot wield the same power as a well-fed, confident man either at home or in the boardroom. If a school in 2020 isn't actively fighting the beauty ideals its students are exposed to then it is simply a different type of 'finishing school' for producing pleasant, adherent young women.

I was shocked when one afternoon that week I posted a photo to Instagram and realised that some of the students I'd spoken to that day were commenting on my account; it was another clashing of worlds. I was some kind of middle step between them and the real glamour-world people like Georgia Fowler who are normally in magazines. At the very least I was a window into young adulthood not limited by the proper-ness their teachers must convcy.

Wolf documented how women's magazines have always followed the shapes and paths of society: Victorian magazines catered to women confined to what was essentially domestic bondage; then, with the First World War pushing women into factories, their remit expanded; then it shrank again when women returned to the home in the 1940s, and so on.

Instagram is to women now what the early, pamphlet-style magazines were back then, particularly in how easily the content is produced and shared. But it is also like glossy magazines in how commercial and perfected it is. When understood as the latest incarnation of fashion and lifestyle media for women, Instagram is also, critically, a reflection of the neoliberal gig economy. Each of us is responsible for our own accounts, our own semi-personal-semi-professional branding. Parents of teenagers are terrified of them having secret second accounts or of posting flirty pictures online. When I finished high school at the end of 2008, most of us had mobile phones but we were a few years away from affordable internet being available through smartphones. I am fortunate enough to be considered a digital native, but I survived the jungle of high school without the terrifying spectre of the smartphone looming over everything I said and did.

A good magazine editor is able to give their readers what they want, accompanied by a nice portion of what they didn't yet realise they wanted. This alertness to the zeitgeist must be married to the objectives of their advertisers (or during wartime, as Wolf noted, the government) and this makes them an incredibly powerful tool for both good and evil. Editors as taste-makers can help catapult society into a sexual revolution, and they can lead us like lemmings over a cliff to starve ourselves in a land of unprecedented plenty; some titles do both. I was infuriated on reading *The Vogue Factor* and *Tongue in Chic* by Kirstie Clements, the former editor of *Vogue Australia*. Both books (the latter sold as fiction but clearly drawn from her experiences at the helm of the glossy fashion title) devote a huge number of pages to describing the bodies of the models, and Clements acted as though she was merely a witness to the starvation in front of her: it was a big damn shame but it was all the designers' fault because their fit models were too small. Tired of being blamed for damaging women's self-esteem, Clements argued that a negative attitude towards fashion 'speaks volumes about a person's self-esteem' and insisted that 'visually, clothes fall better on a slimmer frame'.

In 2014 the Australian fashion designer Alex Perry got slammed for sending an extremely thin model down the catwalk, and he apologised. Various fashion editors and journalists joined the pile-on, using the opportunity to wash their hands of the overwhelmingly underweight standards they had been and would continue to promote in their own publications and advertisements. Two years later another ultra-thin model in an Alex Perry show was singled out for criticism. This time Perry was adamant he had nothing to do with the casting. In his opinion, models that thin shouldn't be allowed to walk the shows. It's mind-blowing how everyone always says someone else is responsible; the buck stops nowhere.

I find it extremely uncomfortable to confront the undeniable fact that Dries Van Noten talks big about designing for a certain kind of bold, intellectual woman but then encourages the same stupid skinny ideal in every single one of his shows. How can his vision for feminine intelligence and strength not extend to the models who wear his designs? His hypocrisy makes me uncomfortable because I recognise it in myself, and he's one of the most intellectual designers alive and working today.

When we curate our own images on Instagram we can set our own agendas but so many of our feeds now present the same ironic conflict that most magazines share—we celebrate our 'empowerment' and 'achievements' while reminding ourselves and each other of the beauty standards which must represent that success, and we conflate the two to the point that they are inextricable. Most cover girls are beautiful *and* meritorious, and sometimes they are only beautiful, but certainly they are never *only* meritorious. Dior produces t-shirts with the slogan WE SHOULD ALL BE FEMINISTS but only sends them to their approved list of toeing-the-line influencers. 'While the editors take a step forward for themselves and their readers, they must also take a step back into the beauty myth for the sake of their advertisers,' Wolf wrote almost three decades ago, and nothing has changed. The joke is on us, though, on people like me, consumers and starry-eyed hopefuls. We mere punters are beholden to these beauty standards when we edit and filter our own feeds; most of us just don't get paid for it. Wolf reflected on a 1950s magazine marketer's report on how best to promote domestic products to predominantly housewife readers. They suggested identifying the products with 'spiritual rewards' and an almost 'religious' feeling or belief. In other words, an ethical ideal. Those are words from an age ago, when 'finishing schools' were the norm, but the products today's girls are being sold are still sold to them with promises of spiritual rewards. That's why more than half of them already know 'good' food from 'bad' food by the time they turn seven and consider dieting. We are doing this to them. I am almost 30—Wolf's generation did it to me.

The year I was born she wrote about the '450 full-time American fashion models who constitute the elite corps deployed in a way that keeps 150 million American women in line'.

As Sebastian Smee wrote in his Quarterly Essay, *Net Loss: The inner life in the digital age*, 'the software knows how to make us want it'. The platforms are tools that act on the users; they do not simply remain passive. Indeed, we are 'being humiliated by it. And betrayed.' Smee quoted Facebook's first president, Sean Parker, and other big names from Silicon Valley, who feel guilty about what they've created and don't let their children use social media at all. We wait to see the stats on our posts because we have a kind of nebulous but firm feeling that we are providing value to some 'unspoken larger social enterprise' when we take part in the digital world. The overlords of these places are profit-driven and often blatantly evil, and sometimes it isn't really an option to just delete your accounts.

They are how we interact with each other, how we find out about cultural movements and the news. Many people do find ways to curate their feeds so that they only show body-positive and food-positive results, but this is not the norm.

I am one of the oldest people to still be considered a digital native and my cohort is much more responsible for keeping each other in line than any generation before us. The democratisation of fashion imagery has given us the tools to define beauty for ourselves, but we are still too fragile, licking our wounds from a history of second-class citizenry, to take the reins handed to us. I followed Skinny Bitch Collective because what *The Beauty Myth* described is still relevant today: 'The modern neuroses of life in the female body spread to woman after woman at epidemic rates', and now the epidemic is literally deadlier than ever. Wolf's chapter on 'Hunger' comes halfway through the book. I had already been shocked when applying her

111

reflections on beauty ideals generally to weight specifically, but on hunger Wolf was painfully precise. A woman starving herself is 'merely doing too well what she is expected to do very well in the best of times'. Starvation is simply the perfection of the specific type of 'greatness' women are currently allowed to aspire to.

Wolf referred to the 'One Stone Solution', an idea that so many girls and women then and now share: that if they could simply lose around 6 kilograms they would be 'their ideal self'. We don't lose these kilograms, though, and so we are all trapped in an awful belief that we can therefore never realise our full potential. 'The inevitable cycles of failure ensured by the One Stone Solution create and continually reinforce in women our uniquely modern neurosis.' We are stuck on this literal and metaphorical treadmill, forever sweating and crying, never quite getting there, or indeed anywhere. A 2016 study from the *Journal of Personality and Social*

Psychology called 'Age and Gender Differences in Self-Esteem: A cross-cultural window' surveyed the majority of literature on self-esteem and 'A robust finding to emerge from this literature is a significant gender gap such that males tend to report higher levels of self-esteem than females do. This gender gap emerges in adolescence and persists throughout early and middle adulthood before it narrows and perhaps even disappears in old age.'

The damage done by eating disorders should be undeniable, but as it is constantly dismissed and patronised, it is, in effect, denied. A commonly cited statistic is that men commit suicide much more than women, but if deaths associated with eating disorders were also considered a different would emerge. In May 2018 the ABC reported that anorexia has the highest death rate of all psychiatric illnesses. Clinical psychologist and past President of the Australia & New Zealand Academy for Eating Disorders Chris Thornton was quoted saying 'more patients with anorexia are likely to commit suicide than patients with a diagnosis of depression'. 'The psychological effects of self-inflicted semistarvation are identical to those of involuntary semistarvation,' Wolf explained with reference to numerous studies. 'The starving body cannot know it is middle class.' The website for Eating Disorders Victoria cites research showing that approximately 20 per cent of females in Australia have an undiagnosed eating disorder and that eating disorders are the third most common chronic illness in young women. 'A Sydney study of adolescents aged 11 to 15 reported that 16% of the girls and 7% of the boys had already employed at least one potentially dangerous method of weight reduction, including starvation, vomiting and laxative abuse.' A study at the University of Sydney in 2007 of nearly 9000 adolescents showed one in five teenage girls starved themselves or vomited up their food to control their weight. I was a teenager in 2007 and wasn't vomiting then, but would start soon after as I felt like a constant and monumental failure.

•

I WILL NEVER forget watching the Amy Winehouse documentary *Amy*, directed by Asif Kapadia. 'What the fuck?' I said to my friends when the lights came on in the cinema. 'Her eating disorder killed her as much as the substances. Did they just not fucking deal with that?'

Photos and videos from Amy's younger years were full of warmth, and her whole body and face looked different. Even the images on her first and second album covers depict starkly different body shapes, and the first album cover shot was taken well after her disordered eating habits began. There is footage of Jane Winehouse, Amy's mother, talking to the camera about when Amy described her 'great new diet' where

115

she would eat and then vomit so she didn't gain weight. When Jane told Amy's father, Mitch, he too dismissed it as trivial. It was a 'phase', a silly-teen-girl thing. This content only appeared halfway through the film, by which time the audience has heard plenty about Amy's alcohol and drug use. Later, someone who worked with her while she was recording *Back to Black* made a reference to Winehouse 'redecorating the bathroom' after eating a meal. Apparently it was only at this point that those around her realised something was 'really' wrong—but I didn't believe that for a millisecond. Winehouse's bulimia had clearly been growing more severe for years, and as she became thinner she sold more records and her fame soared. The documentary was full of people—her father among them—leeching off Winehouse's money and fame, going so far as to sabotage her attempts to get clean and withdraw from public if it meant

postponing money-making tour dates. I found

an article in *Pitchfork* by Kayleigh Hughes in which she shared my frustrations, noting that 'the disease is treated as incidental and almost, to my perception, as something as permanent and untreatable as late-stage cancer, with an air of *nothing can be done*'. The great irony is that while Winehouse went into rehab for drug and alcohol use, sometimes independently and some-times via an intervention, nobody thought to get her into rehab for her blatant bulimia.

When Winehouse survived her first close call, people (including a doctor) referred to her 'petite' frame as putting her at risk from substance over-doses, but we all saw what she looked like when she was a teenager, and it wasn't 'petite'. She had generous breasts and thighs, and there was a solidness to her shoulders and arms coming around a big acoustic guitar. Winehouse's cause of death was officially recorded as 'alcohol pois-oning', but sustained eating disorders damage the body to the point where it can no longer process food or drink properly. A doctor interviewed at the end of the documentary did refer to the 'weakened state of her body', but the focus of the entire film was still on the substance abuse. Vomiting isn't terribly rock-and-roll. It's a high-profile example of how hard it is to track the impact of eating disorders on other officially listed causes of death, but it's also a powerful case study of how disordered eating is dismissed. It is so easy to point to women's fatness as a problem, but thinness can literally kill us and even then not be properly addressed.

•

HOME AGAIN, AND with most of the intense part of the tour finally finished, I sat for a week to consider what I'd learned. I knew that if there were scales in the bathroom I would want to step on them, and I would wonder if I was a failure for not doing so. I would have to exercise constant vigilance to keep a rein on the 'beauty' piece of my self-esteem pie. Even harder than that, I had to begin the lifelong journey of compartmentalising the pieces: regardless of how I felt about my appearance, only deliberate choices of thoughts and attitudes would ensure my sense of self-worth was independent of my body. 'Observe how man's disquiet is all of his own making, and how troubles come never from another's hand, but like all else are creatures of our own opinion,' Aurelius wrote, but he never had to deal with infinite, tiny, needling attacks on his appearance. Stoicism wasn't drafted with social media in mind. Still, I had learned from Widdows and Mair that the ideals couldn't hurt me unless I internalised them. It was like *A Nightmare on Elm Street*—the danger can't hurt you unless you believe in it, but once you do, it grows stronger and more dangerous until someone dies.

My boyfriend was doing a kind of spring clean while I was revisiting *Meditations*, and so

I got up from my desk and walked to the bathroom, picked up the scales, carried them to the
balcony outside the front door and threw them
over the side into the open wheelie bin below.
Then I stared at them, mixed with the kitchen
rubbish and the guinea pig shit, and I smiled.

Unaware that I was out for retribution,
my mobile phone pinged at me from my back
pocket, my fitness app reminding me to 'hop on
the scales!' and update my weight, and there was
a notification about a new video SBC had posted
to Instagram. I deleted the fitness app. I unfol-
lowed SBC. With a taste for blood, I strode into
the bedroom and spent over an hour filling
bags with clothes that didn't fit me comfort-
ably. Each rejected garment was a small but
tactile liberation.

Mair, citing researchers from positive psychology, explained that 'specific garments hold
symbolic meanings of meaningful memories'
and 'even though an item of clothing was no

longer being worn, it was kept as it had transcended its utilitarian function and instead acted as a nostalgic connector to memories'. If you keep the jeans you used to fit into, you're trapping yourself in purgatory—attached to the recollection of a slimmer past self, and resolutely committing to the aspirational future self. I picked up some old skinny jeans and felt that guilt in my gut because of the size of my gut, knowing that I didn't fit into them anymore. I paid attention to that feeling, and then said, 'Fuck off', to the jeans and put them in the bag for recycling. Jeans are inanimate objects that only come to life when you gift them your legs. The only power they have is what you give them, and when you put them in the bin you will see them for what they are: denim tubes. I dumped the bags into piles for recycling or donation and thought to myself that Aurelius might have been proud if he didn't hate women so much.

121

I must project the things I want others to see in me and it has to be a dual message: I am beautiful at any weight, and my beauty isn't what defines me anyway. It's not enough just to disregard the body, for that is also disdain and disowning. I must actually *like* my body. I have taken for granted how I can run and jump, lift things, eat without fear of allergy, and play with dogs. Learning to respect my body was going to take the same practice and patience it took to learn to drive: several years and a few different teachers, and a determination to make that incredible learned skill a seamless part of adult life. At Kmart I bought some new pairs of underpants that were size 12 instead of size 10, and I was grinning like a maniac, because I couldn't have done that before. To do so would have been admitting failure, admitting defeat, giving up, being lazy and worthless. Before, when I didn't have the language I do now, I couldn't have articulated why I felt abandoned when I stopped the churning. Getting dressed in the morning was a masochistic ritual in which I didn't fit into half of my clothes, maintaining a steadfast loyalty to that second self. Now, when I go running, it is because I like myself and there is such joy in the motion. Now, when I am challenged, and I see that aspirational Bri, the one who copes and strives, instead of placing her on a precarious pedestal, I pull her towards me, I close the distance, and I know it is *this* struggle, this wrangling, that I will perfect.

•

IN TRUTH, CASES of obviously diagnosable anorexia and bulimia are no longer what I seek to understand. The perfectionist in me can see the hospital bed option and empathise with it. I've known enough young women who've gone there and envied them their resolve even more than their boniness. Now I'm much more interested in exploring the half-step back from that end of the

123

scale; I want to know why so many of us would never admit to how much time and effort we spend monitoring, tweaking and adjusting our intakes and outputs. Not enough to be hospitalised, but regularly making unhealthy choices because we don't like our bodies.

We are wasting precious time and mountains of money on commercially ritualised self-loathing disguised as 'self-care'. We like the 'body work' because we're taught that it demonstrates commitment to ourselves and communicates class. The most mundane manifestations of this shared malaise are sometimes the most heartbreaking to me. What wonderful meals do we deny each other when we use hurtful language about ourselves in front of our friends? 'Today is my "cheat" meal day', and, 'I exercised today so I've already worked this off.' It is impossible to be ashamed of fatness without inadvertently fat-shaming others, and how many ice creams and sleep-ins with loved ones have you forgone

124

accordingly? 'Complaining to one's friends and family about one's appearance, body size, weight and fear of becoming fat can negatively impact feelings about the self,' Mair wrote: 'Women of all ages and body sizes feel pressure to be self-critical about their bodies. More women than men report exposure to fat-talk and greater pressure to engage in it.' We transmute this gentle self-loathing to our mothers with each application of anti-wrinkle, age-fighting and under-eye cream, and to our children with every mention of being a 'good girl' for avoiding 'bad foods'. There is no way someone can compliment my figure without ultimately harming me by reminding me that my appearance is important and that I am always either getting better or getting worse. If I am getting better, it is a commitment to the second self by disavowing my present self, and if I am getting worse then I am a moral failure undeserving of admiration on any front.

I want to remember the most fun parts of beauty and fashion—of the colours and textures, of the art, the self-expression—instead of accidentally conflating them with whether or not I am 'beautiful'. Now when I see women who I believe look good, I tell them I think they have 'great style'. Style is learned and a joyous source of self-expression that often deliberately bucks certain traditional beauty trends. I no longer admire 'no-make-up make-up' or 'natural beauty' more than I admire wild eyeshadows and bright red lips. I do not compliment a friend who has lost weight. I do not put myself down in front of other people. I don't want to contribute to someone else's internalised self-loathing.

One afternoon in the middle of my semi-starvation regime I was at a restaurant and a very large woman sat down at a table near me. She was beautifully dressed and groomed, and was eating dumplings and ordering champagne by the flute at 3 pm. She wore sparkling pink

nail polish. From this information I determined she enjoyed her life and was accustomed to
doing precisely as she pleased. I liked that and
I warmed to her immediately, but I also feared
that if I too did exactly what I wanted I would
end up big like her. *That must mean I don't like her
body*, I thought, and knew that was a cruel, bad
thing to think. At the time I believed that if I
was fat I would respect myself less, but I also
believed fat people deserved respect, and it was
logically untenable that those thoughts could
coexist in my mind. One had to be a lie. One
had to fail.

•

EARLY SEPTEMBER MEANT New York Fashion
Week. I no longer followed any of the SBC
models on Instagram, but their faces were filling
my feed because the magazines were sharing
the news about who had been chosen to walk the
Victoria's Secret show for 2018. Georgia Fowler

was full of excitement and gratitude at being invited to walk her third show. 'Thank you for seeing my dedication and realising my dream once again,' she wrote in a post where she's smiling, abs rock hard, leaning towards a cab. It made me mad that I'd received this information and would subsequently never be able to forget it, compared to how difficult I found it to remember the capital cities of countries in Europe. I went down a rabbit hole into a strange part of the internet where people criticised models who were cast for the show for not 'deserving' it or not being 'sexy enough'. I was baffled, and it reminded me of why I couldn't stand to watch the Olympics. 'All those people worked so hard, they should *all* win gold!' I yelled at the television, crying, when the women's 200-metre sprints finished. Imagine being selected to walk in a Victoria's Secret show and finding the pocket of the internet filled with thousands of people who don't like your hair enough or think you're just 'not cut out for the wings', whatever that meant. At least in the Olympics the metrics are undeniable. You could spend your entire working life trying to grow more beautiful, and still never know whose version of 'beautiful' to trust. Being booked for shows and campaigns are the markers for successful models—so do their own personal ideas of beauty always align with those of their industry? A sprinter can't have a different definition of 'fast'. And what role did social media play in all that? The comments of thousands of adoring fans—'congratulations' and 'I love you' and 'I'm so happy I'm crying for you'—can't mean nothing. Being regrammed by *Vogue* can't mean nothing. Instagram was the convergence. The party we were all invited to: the editors, designers, companies, customers, models, readers, women and girls. Simultaneously a democracy and a dictatorship.

Eventually airlifting myself out of that absurd grotto, I jumped across to the *New York Times*, trying to replace that brain space with important information. A CGI-rendered image of a model walking through Central Park caught my eye as I was scrolling through their feed. It was Ashley Graham, the first 'curvy' model ever to appear on the cover of *Sports Illustrated* and an advocate for curvy representation in fashion. If I was viewing the story (headlined UNFILTERED) on an iPhone, I'd be able to engage with the virtual reality element of the image. They used 100 cameras to record Graham from all different angles and built an exact replica (no nips or tucks) computer model hologram of her walk, and transplanted it into lots of different places around New York City. It was mesmerising to watch. Graham wore a tight tan top, and there was a gap where it finished at her midriff and where her short, tight white skirt began. Within this tube of a skirt her steps were small, and when she turned you could see where her thighs came out after the curve of her buttocks finished. When she stuck a pose, one hand to her face, the other on her hip, it was a bold move made by soft, bowing lines. I watched it for over ten minutes, this walk of hers, in Central Park, in the New York Botanical Garden, at the Metropolitan Museum of Art, and I was smiling. It was just like LaFever's study of 3D modelling. That was what made the apparition of Graham so arresting—it was undeniable. In the accompanying interview she talked about how early in her career she would be photoshopped and airbrushed without permission, and she was too green to do anything about it. 'Now, I've done many photo shoots where I look over the photographer's shoulder and say, "Don't retouch that. Do not take that out. Keep that in,"' she said, before going on to explain the strange gap in the market between ultra-thin and positively curvy. She explained that 'straight-sized' models are sizes 0 to 4, curvy models are 12 to 16, but there weren't any jobs for the in-betweeners.

That's me now: an in-betweener. I walked to my bedroom, took off my clothes and stepped in front of the mirror again. My heart rate didn't increase the way it had before. A distinct softening had settled over my body since its leanness in June, and at first I thought, *I don't care.* But then, of course, I remembered that wasn't enough; I had to like it. Wolf wrote, 'To enlist young women, we'll need to define our self-esteem as political: to rank it, along with money, jobs, child care, safety, as a vital resource for women that is *deliberately* kept in inadequate supply.' I had run 5 kilometres that morning. My body was marvellous. My fists clenched at the thought of how many years I'd spent drinking the Kool Aid and nothing else. How greatness only ever looked like one thing, and I believed it, and perpetuated it.

•

IN MARCH 2019 the man behind Skinny Bitch Collective, Russell Bateman, posted some videos to their Instagram stories that depicted his exclusive workout group on a 'Kenyan fitness retreat' where the ponytailed, mostly white women used local Kenyan women as props for their drills. The footage is colonialist and cringe-inducing. One of my favourite Instagram accounts, Diet Prada, who are famous for calling out copycat designs but also racism, homophobia, and other miscellaneous bullshit going on in the industry, started sharing the content to their million followers, and within hours the SBC account had been marked 'private', then a couple of days later it was gone completely, and their website taken down. Bateman issued an apology for the insensitivity, but it brought his whole account into focus, and people started looking at the captions on his old posts more carefully. 'NEWSFLASH!' one read. 'Looking and feeling sick, tired, fat, or weak is not an option, and you were not meant to be that way.' His interview content was sifted through, and

I read that he'd once said, 'There's nothing interesting for me about making someone who's overweight a little bit less overweight. The challenge is getting someone who already looks great into epic shape.' It is now shocking to me that at one point in time, relatively recently, I had volunteered to get push notifications every time Russell Bateman posted to that account. How could I have given this man so much of my mental real estate?

When considering a woman's prerogative to use her appearance for her benefit, Wolf wrote with wit and understanding. 'Is she doing her duty to herself, in a clear-eyed appraisal of a hostile or indifferent milieu, by taking care to nourish her real gift under the protection of her incidental one? Does her hand shape the lipstick into a cupid's bow in a gesture of free will?' I try to present a polished package so that people can't dismiss my thoughts about legislative reform. When I don't wear make-up or adhere to certain minimum standards, people (after asking me if I'm sick or tired) either discredit me or don't give a shit about what I have to say. It's like some people can't hear the words coming out of a woman's mouth unless that mouth is covered in Kiss Me Kwick shade 48. According to Wolf, until women are considered equals and have equal power at work, we cannot demonise those of us who use our looks to our advantage in an attempt to level the playing field. I'm not sure how I feel about that. I don't want other emerging authors to see my designer dresses and blow-dried photo shoots and think their book won't sell if they don't do that 'body work' too. Authors should be allowed to be as low-maintenance as they please. Actually, everyone should be allowed to be as low-maintenance as they please. We will never stop recognising 'beauty' in all its varying forms, and nor should we, because true conceptions of beauty celebrate our individuality and choices of expression, but we can stop the halo effect if we truly want to. In the almost 30 years since *The Beauty Myth* was published, our collective 'minimum' standards have grown much more stringent and demanding. Procedures that once seemed extreme are now normal, especially subtle ones fighting ageing like chin tucks and eyelid lifts. On ageing creams and airbrushing, Wolf wrote, 'This issue is not trivial. It is about the most fundamental freedoms: the freedom to imagine one's own future and to be proud of one's own life.' What would I be saying to the older women in my life if I started paying for such procedures? Things we choose for ourselves, things we spend time and money on, tell the people around us what we value.

In the final chapter of *The Beauty Myth* Wolf clarified: 'I am not attacking anything that makes women feel good; only what makes us feel bad in the first place.' So much can be understood by recognising today's trappings of 'beauty' as analogous to the domestic trappings of 'wife and mother' that proliferated in the 1950s. By critiquing these images of perfection I'm not trying to criticise those women who enjoy succeeding at the game, but so many of us, in so many ways, undeniably contribute to the normalisation of the ever-increasing minimums. Some people are born into a privilege of aligning with what their time and place calls 'beauty' and others are not. The women whose interests genuinely align with the practices that others feel trapped and judged by are not to blame. We are in the panopticon. We must tear down the guard, not the other prisoners.

•

ON 9 NOVEMBER 2018 Vanessa Friedman wrote an article for the *New York Times* titled: 'Victoria's Secret Is Trying to Change with the Times. Or Is It?' The show the previous week had displayed a little self-awareness. It opened with a video of the models saying things like, 'We can be sexy for ourselves and who we want to be, not who a man wants us to be', and using words such as 'successful', 'powerful' and 'empowered'. More racially diverse models were sent down the runway than in any previous show. But, as Friedman wrote,

> its essential vocabulary—its approach to the world—is still dedicated to an idea of sexy rooted in the pinup era, when women and their bodies were defined by the eye and imagination of a male beholder; when they were at the mercy of the moguls . . . And that era is on its way to extinction . . . To pretend this is not so is to ignore everything we have learned over the last year about men and women and perception and the danger of received conventions. To think that presenting women as presents to be unwrapped does not shape social expecta-tions is to fool yourself.

Friedman referenced Rihanna's all-inclusive lingerie label Savage x Fenty, which had just showed at New York Fashion Week, as an illustration of the future we might be heading towards: attitude and sex, but on bodies of all shapes and sizes, and with a gaze that had clearly moved past the present-to-be-unwrapped era. Rihanna performed at the 2012 Victoria's Secret show, so the move felt pointed—perhaps even personal—and even though the 2018 Victoria's Secret show had the lowest ratings of all time, it still drew many millions of viewers, so it's hard to see the 'extinction' arriving soon enough. Ed Razek, the 70-year-old chief marketing officer of VS's parent company, told *Vogue* that if they'd done things like Rihanna they would have been 'accused of pandering'. They'd done one plus-sized special in 2000, he added, and nobody was interested, so they didn't plan to revisit sizing diversity. As for whether they should have trans people in the show: 'No. No,

139

I don't think we should . . . Because the show is a fantasy.' He later apologised for the insensitivity and said they would consider casting a trans model.

One of the other frustrating comments Razek made was that over the past two decades the models' body shapes got smaller because the models themselves put pressure on each other. 'Progress gets made, and part of what's happened in our show is that the girls have just continued to get more physically fit. We don't tell them to; they compete with one another and they work hard, they work in pairs, they work in threes. Many of them work out at the same gyms; they have complex routines. They shouldn't have to apologize for that.' It's difficult to know where to begin critiquing the ludicrousness of this statement. The models have to re-audition each year they want to walk in the show, so Razek has clearly misunderstood that he's the one people want an apology from. Georgia Fowler herself once said about her gruelling routines: 'I do it for me. I want to show that I deserve to be there, and have worked hard to be there.' The language of actual empowerment has been completely co-opted. In some kind of freaky Stockholm syndrome, she and the other angels speak with familial warmth about the VS people who support them and give them such incredible opportunities. This is Capitalism 101. The moment we feel we are competing with each other, or the moment we think we're doing it for ourselves, is the moment the big money-making machine has won. Of course the models who earn their thousands of dollars from perpetuating these narrow ideals play a large part, but to find the real seat of power we must ask who is making the millions.

Soon after all that went down I did a big event where people in the signing line told me what a positive impact my book had on their lives, and my friends and I went out for dinner afterwards. When I returned home and undressed I noticed my midsection didn't dip back in after my bottom ribs the way it had before, and I rested my hands on my overfull belly. 'If we are to free ourselves from the dead weight that has once again been made out of femaleness, it is not ballots or lobbyists or placards that women will need first,' Wolf wrote, 'it is a new way of seeing.'

•

THE FINAL LINE of *The Beauty Myth* asked not what we see when we look in the mirror, but what we *decide* to see. 'What *will* we see?' she asked. Yes, I am pressured from all sides, and yes, the enemy can feel like an unknowable, phantom-like omnipresent cloud. But also, I have fought before and I can fight again. The last time I picked a battle it was with a demented system and a broken, brutal man. The lesson in all that was that as soon as you start fighting for yourself you're automatically winning; in a system stacked against you, survival is success. When I look in the mirror now I do have a new way of seeing, and it is just as it was with the last battle; when I thought I couldn't push on for myself, I could push on for others.

'Most urgently,' Wolf wrote about the real damage dealt by these ideas, 'women's identity must be premised upon our "beauty" so that we will remain vulnerable to outside approval, carrying the vital sensitive organ of self-esteem exposed to the air.' This is the first step: reducing the size of the 'beauty' piece of my pie. And how true, that self-esteem is a vital organ. For me now, beauty will be a hobby, like playing the clarinet or my occasional forays into painting. Enjoyable precisely because I have no intention of trying to perfect the pursuit. Full of colour and self-expression, ever-changing, fun because it is without pressure.

What do I now believe is the perfect body for me? One that talks and loves and runs, eating what I want to fuel my relationships and adventures. And if this body happens to be 65 kilograms or 70 or more, then that must be perfect too. I can will it so. At one point near the end of *Meditations* Aurelius inexplicably slipped into feminine articles and pronouns: 'The soul attains her perfectly rounded form when she is neither straining out after something nor shrinking back into herself; neither disseminating herself piecemeal nor yet sinking down in collapse; but is bathed in a radiance which reveals to her the world and herself in their true colours.'

I am tired of teenagers shrinking back into themselves. I do not want my mother to sink down in collapse. I want to see my friends bathed in radiance. And so I must reveal my true self to the world.

Acknowledgements

How LUCKY I am that I always have so many people to thank!

First, as always, thank you Mum and Dad. Sorry I keep writing about grizzly things. None of the pressures I documented in this essay came from you, and you both always look for what's on the inside of people. I greatly admire and appreciate the example you set for me in this and all things.

Jane Palfreyman, you are the greatest publisher a girl could ever ask for (so badass and kind) and you make me very proud to be part of the Allen & Unwin family. Grace Heifetz, agent extraordinaire, I am so very excited for you. Both the near and distant future are looking mighty bright, and I'm stoked to be going with you all the way, every day.

To Tessa Feggans, Ali Lavau, and Kate Goldsworthy: I am incredibly fortunate to have had your time and expertise to help bring *Beauty* into the world. It has been a privilege working with such an experienced, professional and lovely team.

The cover of this book is exactly what I'd hoped for. Huge gratitude to the immensely talented artist Loribelle Spirovski for letting us use this arresting image, and to the design master Lisa White (who also did *Eggy*) and who I hope does every book of mine forevermore.

Thank you, Nkechi, for your generous time and honest insights—I'm so happy I got stood up and we are now friends! To my early readers

Fiona Wright and Grace McCarter, thank you for making space for me in your already word-heavy schedules: your insights were wonderful.

I will never forget how Fiona Stager and Krissy Kneen from Avid Reader Bookstore in Brisbane set me on my writing path. Long before I ever worked there the shop was a kind of guiding star for me. I think of it fondly and often.

This essay was written as part of my MPhil in Creative Writing at the University of Queensland, generously supported with a scholarship from the Australian government and the Alfred Midgley Scholarship. Warm and admiring thanks to my supervisor, Bronwyn Lea, for being so supportive. I leave all our conversations with thoughts and ideas that stay with me for days.

I also benefited from a Brisbane City Council Lord Mayor's Fellowship which sent me to New York City to learn from the best in longform essay writers.

And finally, thank you dear Vincent. Just when I thought we couldn't possibly be any happier, after another year together we've grown even closer, and here I am, a better person for having you in my life each day. The work I am most proud of is the love we share.

Further Reading

REFERENCES

Aurelius, M., *Meditations*, London: Penguin Books, 2004.

Bonham-Carter, D., *Introducing Self-Esteem: A practical guide*, London: Icon Books, 2012.

Clements, K., *The Vogue Factor*, Melbourne: Melbourne University Press, 2013.

Clements, K., *Tongue in Chic*, Melbourne: Melbourne University Press, 2013.

Mair, C., *The Psychology of Fashion*, London: Routledge, 2018.

Mühl, M. & von Kopp, D., *How We Eat with Our Eyes and Think with Our Stomachs: The hidden influences that shape your eating habits*, Melbourne: Scribe, 2018.

Smee, S., *Net Loss: The inner life in the digital age*, Melbourne: Black Inc., 2019.

Storr, W., *Selfie*, Sydney: Picador, 2017.

Valentish, J., *Woman of Substances*, Melbourne: Black Inc., 2017.

Widdows, H., *Perfect Me: Beauty as an ethical ideal*, New Jersey: Princeton University Press, 2018.

Wolf, N., *The Beauty Myth*, London: Vintage, 1991.

OTHER RECOMMENDED READING

Gay, R., *Hunger*, New York, NY: HarperCollins, 2017.

Heti, S., Julavits, H., Shapton, L. et al., *Women in Clothes*, New York: Blue Rider Press, 2014.

Lanier, J., *Ten Arguments for Deleting Your Social Media Accounts Right Now*, Sydney: Bodley Head, 2018.

Moss, T., *The Fictional Woman*, Sydney: HarperCollins, 2014.

West, L., *Shrill*, New York: Hachette Books, 2016.

Wright, F., *Small Acts of Disappearance*, Sydney: Giramondo, 2015.